Lessons Learned

from a

Sitcom Life

by

Karen S. Veazey

To Aunt Vesta who inspired me

to write this book.

and

To my two girls who gave me so

much to write about.

Table of Contents

Introduction

As a child I watched a lot of situation comedies on the television. They were all reruns from the 50's, 60's, and 70's. One of my favorite sitcoms was *Green Acres,* and my favorite character on that show was Lisa Douglas, played by Eva Gabor. Although Lisa Douglas was rather ditzy, I really wanted to be like her when I grew up. She was so sophisticated yet kind, and not even the local "nuts" could ruffle her feathers.

Speaking of feathers, she also had those gorgeous peignoir sets. That is probably what I liked best about her. I loved her fancy 60's clothes.

Although I still do not own any peignoir sets, I have turned out to be like Lisa Douglas in a few ways. I have her cooking skills. (Remember the really thick coffee and the bubbling pancakes?) My house is always a mess, because we always have several home improvement projects going on at the same time. Because I am always working on some home improvement project, I spend many of my days in my painting clothes, with no makeup, and my hair not fixed. The only paint on my nails is what is splattered on them while painting a room. For these reasons, I have come to the conclusion that I grew up to be less like Lisa Douglas and more like another character on *Green Acres*. Yes, I have become Ralph, the female painter. Like Ralph, I am always painting something, yet the house does not seem to look any better.

Green Acres is not the only show that has had an impact on whom I became as an adult. I could go on and on about *The Lucy Show, The Flying Nun, Gilligan's Island, Leave it to Beaver, The Munsters, The Brady Bunch,* and *The Partridge Family.* One thing these sitcoms have in common is that they all concluded each episode with the lesson the viewer should have learned from the show. The lessons I learned, however, were not usually the ones intended by the shows' writers. In fact, I have noticed that the lessons I learn in real life are often very different from the deductions of others. This book is all about lessons I have learned from this reality sitcom called "Life".

Part I

Chapter 1

Pets and Big Brothers

The Smell of New Upholstery

My family has always been a pet family. When I was really young, we had a dog named Lambsie. (Yes, my parents let us children name her.) Lambsie loved to dig holes under our fence, so she could chase our milkman. The milkman eventually refused to come to our house anymore until we got rid of "that dog". Well Lambsie possibly chased other people as well, because we found her poisoned one day. By this time, the milkman no longer delivered milk in our neighborhood, so he was not our prime suspect.

It was during this time of bereavement that my Uncle Bill and Cousins Billy and Johnny from Arkansas came to visit. With them they brought their favorite cat, Anastasia. They stayed several days with us, and a good time was had by all. When it came time to leave, Anastasia could not be found. We promised to take care of her if she returned, and somehow we would return her to them.

I am sure my mom was thinking, "How long am I going to be stuck with this cat, and how on earth am I getting her back to Arkansas?" If they had pet taxis back then, we did not know about them. Traveling long distances with a small animal loose in the car was not my mom's idea of fun.

A few days went by and still there was no sign of that cat. Then we received a call from a very angry neighbor. On his way to work that morning, he started to get into his car, and guess who he saw? Yes, Anastasia and her two new kittens. She had given birth to her little miracles on the fabric upholstery of his brand new car. Unfortunately, he hated and was allergic to cats. Judging from the yelling and cursing that was spilling out of the phone and into my father's ear, I guessed the neighbor was not crazy about a baby-birthing mess being in his car either.

My father apologetically collected the cat and kittens from our neighbor. It was our first litter of kittens, and they were adorable. One was a yellow striped kitten we named Tiger. The other kitten was a striped cream colored kitten that we named Tigger.

This was the beginning of a new stage in my brother's and my childhood. We now had cats.

Anastasia did make it back to Arkansas, but my uncle must have come back to Tennessee to get her. No one in the family can really remember.

Lesson Learned: If your neighbor's pregnant cat goes missing, don't leave your car windows down.

Fur and Water Do Not Mix

I have only one sibling, my older brother Jerry. When we were growing up, Jerry was the mischievous one of the two of us. At least that's the way I remember it. Aggravation was my brother's greatest joy. It did not matter if he was tormenting me, my parents, his teachers, or others. He was always thinking up new ways to aggravate someone. It was never anything too bad; it was just bad enough to amuse himself and maybe a friend or two.

One day, Jerry must have decided he had not aggravated our kittens Tiger and Tigger enough, so he came up with a "great idea" and convinced me to take part in his plan. My job was to hold the kittens while he sprayed them with the water hose.

I knew cats hated getting wet, so Jerry's idea sounded funny. I did not, however, think the scenario through like I should have.

We rounded up the cats, and I held them as directed. I still had not grasped the consequences of this plan, but they quickly became apparent. First, I had not thought about how wet I would get. That concern quickly left me, though, once the kittens started clawing their way up my body, onto my head, down my back, and finally down my legs. My brother followed them with the hose as they climbed me like a scratching post.

Afterward, I looked like I had the starring role in *Carrie*. When my brother quit laughing, he begged, "Don't tell Mom! Don't Tell Mom!" I didn't have to tell Mom, as it turns out. My scratches did the talking for me.

Lesson Learned: Get away from your brother when he has "a good idea".

Baton Practice

Tiger and Tigger were sweet, playful kittens. I spent a lot of time playing in our backyard with them. I also spent a lot of time practicing my baton twirling. My mom would not let me take twirling lessons, which I could not understand. After all, I was only taking dancing lessons, piano lessons, choir, Girls in Action....Anyway, on one such day, I was in the backyard practicing a baton routine that I had made up myself. I did my routine to Barry Manilow's tune *I write the Songs*. This was back when this song was new and there was no such thing as a portable boom box, which meant I had to sing the song myself while performing my baton routine. Being the ripe old age of 7 or 8 years old, singing and twirling a baton at the same time required great concentration. This is why I probably did not notice Tigger jumping at the baton on one of its downward swings. I looked down just in time to see the baton's rubber end smack the kitten in the head.

That smack knocked the cat out! I thought I had killed him, but then I could see he was breathing. "Mom and Dad can't find out about this." I told myself. "They'll fuss at me for not paying attention to what I was doing. They'll take my baton away from me, and, even worse, they will get rid of the kittens."

I came up with a plan. I would doctor the cat myself. No one would know. I snuck into the house and found a vitamin bottle. Back then, each bottle came with a funny looking capsule in it. The capsules were full of tiny little white balls. Mom would not let me touch them, so I knew they had to be powerful medicine. (Now I know that these were silicon capsules that were put into the bottles to absorb moisture.)

I grabbed one of the capsules and snuck back outside. I took it apart and mixed it in my hand with some water. I picked up the kitten. He was still lifeless, but was finally conscious. I tried to feed the concoction to the kitten. To my frustration, Tigger would not eat it. I kept telling him, "This will make you feel better." Thank goodness the cat had more sense than I did. Eventually he got annoyed at me trying to "help" him, and he decided to get down. I was very relieved that I had not killed the cat, and that the cat could not tattle on me.

After a few days, my brother, came into the kitchen and said, "Has anyone noticed Tigger's head? His forehead looks flat."

I went out to look at Tigger. I was bewildered at the sight. I suppose I was too young to understand the cause and effect concept. We had never had a kitten before, so my brother and I concluded that that must be the way kittens looked when their skulls grew. Tigger's head was just changing shape.

I didn't put two and two together until years later: The baton, the flat forehead…poor kitty.

Lesson Learned: Batons, Barry Manilow, and kittens are a bad combination.

Ketchup Can Be Misleading

This brother of mine had a best friend, Greg, who lived down the street from us. Greg was a sweet boy who could be easily swayed by my brother to act otherwise.

Greg lived on the corner and had a stop sign at the edge of his yard. This gave my brother "a great idea". One hot summer day, the two of them decided to wrap their bikes (banana seats and all) around the stop sign, so it would look like they had had a wreck. Then they went into Greg's house and got the ketchup bottle. They covered themselves in ketchup and intertwined themselves in the "wrecked bikes". They then lay there in waiting.

That ketchup dried quickly in the hot summer sun, but it was worth the stiff discomfort when cars drove by. Several cars stopped to try to help these "poor children". At this point, Greg and Jerry would hop up and say "We're OK. We're OK." Even though several neighbors were hacked off by this stunt, no one called my parents.

Lesson Learned: You can't count on your neighbors to get your brother into big trouble.

Handcuffs Are a Bad Idea

One summer, our babysitter decided we should all walk down the street and pay Greg and his mom a visit. While our sitter and Greg's mom visited, Jerry, Greg and I played outside.

On this particular day, Greg had a great surprise to show Jerry. His older brother was a policeman or some such person and had given Greg a real pair of handcuffs.

This gave my brother another "great idea". We would play "cops and robbers". Guess who the robber was? Yes, it was me, the little baton twirling, ballet dancing girl.

After much chasing, the two of them caught me. They threw me to the ground and handcuffed my hands behind my back. While I was still face down in the dirt, they decided they were bored with this game and ran off to play (Talk about ADHD).

Do you know how hard it is to get off the ground with your hands behind your back and your face in the dirt? This experience probably nipped in the bud any thoughts I might have had of a life of crime. I didn't even think about stepping through my shackled hands, so I could get my hands in front of my body. Instead, I floundered face down on the ground for a while.

When I finally managed to get up and go to the house, I couldn't open the door. (I was not about to look for Jerry and Greg. They would probably cuff me to a tree next.) After banging my body against the metal screen door several times, Greg's mom finally opened the door for me.

I do not remember what was said, but I think the handcuffs were confiscated. Did my brother get in trouble? Once again, no.

Lesson Learned: Never let some guy(s) talk you into wearing handcuffs.

Skates and Dollies

The house I grew up in was in a good size neighborhood. Our house was on a hill, so our driveway had a nice slope to it. This gave my brother endless ideas for creative ways for us to go down that driveway. One method of traveling was with our metal wheeled roller skates. These skates made every inch of your body vibrate as you skated across the asphalt. We would skate on those metal skates until our legs were numb. We would skate down our driveway toward the road, and, just as we were about to skate into the road, we would turn and skate into the yard. Of course, skating on grass does not work very well, so we would usually fall or look like a cartoon character trying to keep his balance while limbs were flying every which way.

We knew better than to go into the street. I had found out the hard way what would happen if we did. I had been riding my bike down the driveway and into the street one day, following Jerry. I meant to turn right, but I must have leaned too far into the turn. My bike and I went sliding across the street and stopped right in front of a little old man's car. He was only going about 5 miles an hour, and stopped in plenty of time to keep from turning me into road kill. However, that is not the story that my brother told my mom. We both had to hear an hour-long lecture on how we should watch for traffic and how we did not need to play in the road. Then Mom punished me. (I always felt that the long lecture should have counted as part of the punishment, but no, not at OUR house.)

When riding down our hilly driveway, we could really build up some speed. Not going into the street prevented us from taking advantage of that added acceleration. That in itself was a tragedy, but facing my mother's wrath if we did go into the street again would have been an even greater tragedy.

After skating down the driveway hundreds of times and crashing into the grass, one Saturday my brother decided that we needed to try something new. He went into the garage to see what contraption he could come up with. Oh, he came up with another "great idea". He brought out our dad's dolly. It was really cool! The dolly had four wheels instead of two, so you could lay it flat on the ground. The handle could be removed and put into a different set of holes. This made the handles stand perpendicular to the dolly and the ground, and this turned the dolly into something like a big cart one might find in a lumber store. My brother then found an old, hard shell suitcase which he placed at the back of the dolly. The suitcase became the seat for our new bobsled on wheels.

We pushed the modified dolly to the top of the driveway. We were still wearing our metal skates. I suppose this was for added speed. One of us sat on the suitcase while the other pulled the dolly, skating as fast as he/she could. Once we got going, the person pulling hopped on the dolly and sat on the suitcase as well. As we got close to the road, we leaned to the right, so the dolly rolled into our grass.

I can guess what you may be thinking: Where were our parents? Well Dad was supposed to watch us on Saturdays while Mom was at work. So, this story is a perfect example of why moms' hearts are filled with fear when they hear a father say that he is "going to watch the children."

Jerry and I continued training for the roller skating bobsled team for many Saturdays until that one fateful day. It was my brother's turn to pull the dolly. I was sitting on the suitcase, but it must not have been positioned quite right. As we sped down the driveway, Jerry hopped on, but the suitcase slid off. I went flying. I do not know what happened to my brother, but my head hit the asphalt with a thud. I was knocked out. When I came to, my brother and two other boys were leaning over me saying, "Don't tell Mom. Don't tell Mom! Promise me you won't tell Mom!" I did not tell. (I later found out there were no other boys there. It turns out that you really do see double or even triple if you hit your head hard enough.)

Lessons Learned: There is no roller skating bobsled team at the Olympics, suitcases should be tied on to dollies, and, if you are knocked unconscious, you should, in fact, tell your mom.

Spiders Are Not For Cuddling

I have a lot of cousins, but there are a few with whom I spent a lot more time. Two of them are Billy and Johnny. Spending time with them was always so much fun. My brother and I hated it when they moved to Arkansas, but we went to visit them as often as we could.

Just walking into Billy and Johnny's house was an adventure. You never knew what you were going to find, or what their newest hobbies would be. During Johnny's exotic animal phase, he had a pet tarantula. To everyone's horror one evening, the tarantula got out of his aquarium somehow. (I honestly had nothing to do with that mishap.) The tarantula was nowhere to be found, which caused quite a panic in the house.

The spider's dead body was found the next morning by my brother and Johnny. The cause of death was never clear. The subject was always changed when I brought it up. I assume death was brought on by a panicked relative.

Johnny put the spider in a big jar of formaldehyde and gave it to my brother. My brother brought the dead spider home to Tennessee and kept that jar on his dresser for years. He was so proud of it.

Lesson Learned: Boys are truly icky.

Playing with Guns

During another family visit to Arkansas, we decided to go target practicing. I was in grade school and had never fired a gun before. Pop and Uncle Bill were with us, but I do not think they were watching my brother, cousins, or me very closely.

Jerry and my cousins were shooting their guns at targets. I saw a shotgun on the ground and decided to give it a try. I asked Johnny for some guidance, but he was too busy to be bothered by his little cousin. I just decided to do what they do in the movies.

I held up the gun. I closed one eye (The wrong eye as it turned out.) and looked down the barrel. I aimed for the target. There was one big problem with my stance, however. The butt of the gun is supposed to be in line with your shoulder. I did not know this. Instead, I had positioned the butt of the gun in line with my face.

I pulled the trigger. The gun kicked back into my front tooth. That kick threw me backward to the ground. I was not sure what happened, but I guessed that something must not have gone right. My front tooth was knocked back just a little, but did not fall out. My cousins looked back at me on the ground as if to say, "Why is she way back there, and why is she on the ground?" Then they turned back around and continued their target practicing.

No, we did not tell Mom.

Lesson Learned: Guns can hurt.

Chapter 2

Bathroom Chaos

Shower Scares

Many years ago my brother got a new water gun. It looked like a real revolver, which was pretty impressive in the 1970's. I decided to fill it up with water and try it out. I headed to the bathroom. The door was closed, and I realized that my mom was in the shower.

My mom always locked the bathroom door when she was in the shower, and I knew that. However, I did not know at the time that she always kept the door locked because of her fear of living out the shower scene from the movie *Psycho*.

Anyway, I tried the door knob and found that the door was unlocked this time. Suddenly I had a change of plans. I decided to squirt Mom with the new water gun. After all, she was already wet. How mad could she get?

I filled the water gun elsewhere in the house and snuck back into the bathroom. I positioned my gun and yanked the shower curtain back in a flash. When my mom saw what looked like a real gun, the screaming began. I started spraying her. After Mom realized the gun was a toy, she - as we say in the south - proceeded to beat the tar out of me with the shower still going. Then began the two-hour lecture on how I better not ever do that again. In the end, I felt like the real victim in this whole shower scene, because nothing is more frightening than a scared, angry, wet, naked momma.

Lesson Learned: If you scare your mom with a water gun, start running sooner!

More Scary Showers

Jerry and I had some Johnny West toys handed down to us when we were kids. I discovered that the saddles for the Johnny West horses fit my kitten, Wally, very nicely. My brother had not yet seen how cute the cat looked wearing a saddle, so I decided he needed to see Wally right that minute. Unfortunately he was in the shower, but I did not let that stop me. I put the saddled kitten in the bathroom with Jerry and shut the door.

Still young and curious, Wally wanted to know what was going on behind that curtain. She jumped into the shower with my brother. You have never heard such a commotion. My brother screamed. The cat screamed, and there were all kinds of banging noises.

After all the noise stopped, I eased the door open, just a bit. There was my poor cat, soaking wet with the seat of the saddle turned upside down on her belly. Her eyes were wide open. By now my brother realized I was in the bathroom. He started fussing at me, so I did what any sister would do. I grabbed the wet cat, went out the door, and left him in the shower fussing to the walls.

Lesson Learned: Let the cat explore the bath tub when your screaming brother is not in it.

Even More Scary Showers

When I was very young, my Aunt Louise bought me a large doll at a yard sale. The doll was taller than I was. She was as heavy as lead and looked like the bride of "Chucky". I did not notice, though. I named her Sissy, probably because of the television show *Family Affair*, and dragged her - literally-everywhere with me. As I got older, my friends complained that the sight of Sissy scared them.

One time I stuck her in my bedroom window so people driving by our house would think she was a real child looking out the window. All was well until my dad drove home from work. He did not recognize Sissy and wanted to know "who that scary kid in the window was." Yes, he made me move her.

As the years went by, I thought about getting rid of Sissy. Somehow my mom always suspected and would ask, "Where is Sissy? You aren't getting rid of her, are you? You cannot get rid of SISSY." I decided to try to give her to my daughters. They didn't want her, but they did not want me to get rid of her, either. I needed to keep her FOREVER, they thought. (Yes, they had been listening to my mom.)

I finally came up with a use for Sissy. You see, one of my bosses was perfect for pulling pranks on. He had a Napoleon complex that he adamantly denied. He seemed to have an ever-constant internal struggle to act macho, but I knew that, if given the chance, he could scream like a little girl.

I had a second boss who could best be described as the gentle giant. My two bosses had a gym and full bathroom in the back of their shop. They worked out and showered, separately I must add, early each morning before their employees came to work.

One day while the two of them were out to lunch, I got Sissy out of the trunk of my car and stood her up in the shower. By design, the next day was my day off. I thought this would give my bosses some cooling-down time if they did not take the prank well. The other employees knew about Sissy and could not wait for the next day to come. They had little to fear. They knew I would immediately be blamed.

As expected, "Napoleon" worked out the next morning and went to shower first. As he started to turn on the water, he pulled back the curtain. As I understand it, girlie screams followed. This sent the "Gentle Giant" running to "Napoleon's" aid. By now "Napoleon" was holding Sissy straight out in front of him trying to figure out what was going on. Why was this doll in his shower? In rushed the "Gentle Giant". He saw naked "Napoleon" holding what he thought was a little girl, so the gentle giant hollered.

Both of my bosses recovered. However, "Napoleon" had to have sufficient time to fuss about the event to the other employees before he could recover completely. Did I get the blame? Yes, but I wouldn't have it any other way.

News about Sissy began to travel. One day my best friend Bobbie gave me a call. She wanted to borrow that doll. Bobbie is the only female in her household, and the thought of a scary doll that looks real gave her many ideas.

Bobbie's first prank was to put Sissy in the shower. That scared her husband, Joe. His knees gave way and he let out with a censored exclamation. Surprisingly Joe did not think the bit was very funny, but he agreed to keep Sissy a secret. Next, Bobbie hid Sissy in her son Jared's closet while he slept. She knew that he would open the closet door first thing in the morning.

The next morning Bobbie sat in the kitchen listening. She heard Jared's alarm clock go off. She heard him slowly walk over to his closet and open the folding doors. She then heard the pitter patter of his 11-year-old feet quickly leaving his bedroom and running up the hall. Jared quickly got over his slight annoyance with his mother and was also sworn to secrecy.

Bobbie's next target was Tanner, her youngest son. One night while Tanner was sleeping, she set Sissy at the foot of his bed. He must not have been completely awake when Bobbie heard him yell, "I don't want it! I don't want it!" The sight of Sissy did not scare him, but the fear that someone had given him a doll sure did.

Lesson Learned: Even after all these years, Sissy is still fun to have around.

Public Restroom Stalls

My mom and I were both in a public restroom one time. We each went to a stall. After a couple minutes, mom said, "I don't have any toilet paper. Would you hand me some?" I tore off what I thought was a generous amount of toilet paper and handed it under the stall wall.

Once again Mom again said, "I need some toilet paper, Karen!" I replied, "Well, reach down and take it." She retorted, "I can't reach it." I stretched a little farther. Mom again said, "Stretch farther. I still cannot reach it." I said, "I cannot stretch any farther. Would you just take it?"

By this point we were getting aggravated with each other, and we started arguing.

"Give me some toilet paper! Is that so much to ask of my own daughter?" fussed my mom. "What do you want me to do, come in there and deliver it?" I replied.

I was really beginning to get tired of how uncomfortable I was, leaning to one side with my arm stretched out as far as it could go. In a very hateful way I finally said, "Get up and take the toilet paper!" Mom answered, "I would if you would hand it to me!"

Suddenly I felt the paper leave my hand. I then heard an unfamiliar giggle coming from the stall beside me. I bent over even farther to look at the shoes next to me.

Those were not my mom's shoes. Our stalls were <u>not</u> next to each other! There was an innocent woman in between us who had spent the whole time in her stall with other people's hands and arms reaching toward her from either side. The poor woman finally decided to just transfer the toilet paper from my hand to Mom's.

When I made this discovery, I proclaimed, "Mom, you are <u>not </u>in the stall next to me." Mom said, "What? Are you kidding me?" "There is a stall between us." I continued. The three of us had a good laugh. The other woman quickly snuck out of the restroom, though. I don't even think she flushed.

Lesson Learned: Don't go to the restroom with my mom.

Bathtub Surprise

After his spider died, my cousin Johnny bought a pet iguana. The best I can remember, the iguana was about two and a half feet long. Johnny's mom, my Aunt Louise, was horrified by the big lizard. Being around him did not bother me too much, except when the lizard ate scrambled eggs. That was just too gross too watch.

Johnny loved his iguana and tried to take good care of him. He thought the iguana might like to wet its skin and take a swim from time to time, so he decided to put some water in the bathtub. Johnny then just left his lizard unattended in the tub and went over to a friend's house.

In the meantime, Aunt Louise needed to use the bathroom. She did not know that the tub was doubling as a swimming pool. The tub was three or four feet away from the toilet. As Aunt Louise was sitting, minding her own business, two reptile paws (do lizards have paws?) moved up the side of the tub. Slowly the iguana raised his head over the side and began glaring at Aunt Louise. She began screaming and then hopped off the toilet and continued hopping out of the bathroom and down the hallway with her pants around her ankles, screaming the whole way.

Aunt Louise feared that the reason the animal was out of his aquarium was that he had figured a way to escape his glass cage. She then did what any mom would do in such a situation. She called animal control and had them take the iguana away within the hour. How did she get animal control to respond so quickly? She was so hysterical; they probably thought Godzilla was on the loose.

Lesson Learned: Aunt Louise would do well in a sack race if an iguana were chasing her.

The Boy's Restroom

Back in eighth grade when I was attending West Middle School, the school planned a talent show. As a joke, several of my friends and I decided to have a jug band and do our own rendition of the Oak Ridge Boy's classic song "Elvira". We decided we would dress up in old overalls and plaid flannel shirts. Each one of us had a homemade instrument. I played the Coke bottles.

The day of the big talent show arrived. I kept going back and forth to the girl's bathroom to put water in my Coke bottles. I was going to great lengths to get each bottle's tone just right. Simply filling a water pitcher with water would have been a good idea. It would have saved me so many trips to the bathroom, but I was too young to be logical.

On one of my many trips, I walked into the bathroom and encountered quite a shocking sight. There at the sinks were two guys dressed up like girls. They had on makeup, wigs, and long dresses. I thought, "They must think that girls are idiots if they think that we would mistake them for girls." What I said was, "What are you doing in here?" They asked, "What are YOU doing in here?" I replied, "Just because you're dressed up like girls does not mean you can use the girl's bathroom."

I was not prepared for their response. "Karen, you're in the boy's bathroom." "Sure," I thought, "they are just trying to confuse me, because I caught them in the girl's room dressed in drag." They were so insistent that I began to wonder if they were telling the truth. The stalls were behind me, and I had not seen any telltale signs that this was a boy's bathroom. After all, it was laid out the same as the girl's restroom. I really began to wonder about their story when another boy not wearing an evening gown walked into the restroom. I opened the door and read the sign: MEN. I turned to the boys and said, "Oh, this IS the boy's room."

I said nothing else and walked away. After all, I needed to hurry up, so I could make an idiot of myself in our jug band. (By the way, the jug band was much funnier in theory than in actuality.)

Lesson Learned: Those boys made really ugly girls.

Chapter 3

Clever Solutions

Halloween Upsets

We had a great friend that lived next door when we were growing up. Her name is Becky. In fact her whole family is great. Their last name is Adams, so we had great fun telling everyone that we lived next door to the Adams Family. I think the TV show was actually new then.

One Halloween, my mom, brother, and I went trick-or-treating with Becky and her mom, Aunt Viola. (In the south, it used to be customary to refer to close friends of the family as "Aunt" or "Uncle", and Viola definitely has "Aunt" status.) Becky, Jerry, and I were each carrying huge paper shopping bags so we would have plenty of room for our Halloween spoils. I was probably only three or four years old at that time and was not quite tall enough to carry my big paper bag with handles, so I was dragging it on the ground. As the night went on, the grass became damp from the dew. I was unaware of what happens to paper bags that are dragged across wet ground.

After visiting one neighbor's house, I happened to look into my bag. In the bottom of that bag was a huge hole, and most of my candy was gone. I was totally shocked, and expressed my disbelief out loud. Becky and Jerry peeked into my bag. They both laughed hysterically. I cried.

Becky's mom wisely said, "You two might as well stop laughing, because you each are going to give Karen HALF of your candy." Then their laughter turned to tears. I stopped crying. I was very young, but I still figured out that I was going to make out better than Becky and Jerry that Halloween. Becky and Jerry fussed the whole way home. Life was as it should be.

Lesson Learned: Aunt Viola Rocks.

Boy Troubles

As fate would have it, the Adams family moved away before I started kindergarten. Now I was the only girl around my house. Not only was my only sibling a brother, but several of my older male cousins were often at my house as well (before and after two of my cousins moved to Arkansas). These boys did not want to play with the "baby" of the family, especially since I was a girl. I was always trying to prove that I could do anything they could do. The only time they paid attention to me, though, was when they wanted to aggravate me. Little did they know that I was taking notes.

I had an imaginary friend named Kathy. Nothing seemed to bother my brother and cousins more than when I talked about Kathy. They would tell me how there was no Kathy. I calmly and smugly would say, "Oh, yes there is." This seemed to drive them crazy, and one of them would run off and tattle to my mom or to Aunt Louise (also known as my second mom), but I do not remember ever being fussed at about Kathy. I do not even remember being accused of lying by my two moms. I suspect that my being outnumbered by boys occasionally worked to my advantage when it came to leniency.

The story of my elusive friend was beginning to get less and less feasible, though. Since my brother and cousins were constantly around, one of them would have surely seen her. I knew that I would have to eventually confess the whole thing to these boys who tormented my life.

One day however, when my brother, my cousins Billy and Johnny, and I were in the backyard, I noticed a young girl two houses down from ours. I had never seen her before, so I figured she was just visiting Mr. Mullins, who lived in that house. Billy, Johnny, and Jerry had just been arguing with me about Kathy. I suddenly had a great idea. I went to the edge of our yard and called, "Hi Kathy!" and gave her a big wave. To my delight, the girl responded with a big wave, but said nothing. I did not say anything to Billy, Johnny, or Jerry. Instead, I pretended not to notice them while I examined something on the ground and listened to their reaction. They started talking among themselves in very shocked tones. It was GREAT!

Luckily, "Kathy" did not come over and tell us her real name. I never brought up the subject of my imaginary friend again. I did not want to push my luck.

Lesson Learned: Boys are really gullible.

That Darn Cat

After the Adams family moved away, we got new neighbors, The Jacobs. My brother and I were very unhappy about this. Little did we know that our unhappiness would grow exponentially. Not only did the Jacobs not have children or grandchildren, Mrs. Jacobs did not like children. Paradoxically, even though she did not like children, Mrs. Jacobs was a piano teacher. My mom thought this was wonderful. Jerry and I could take piano lessons without having to be driven anywhere. All we had to do was walk next door. Well, I am not going to go into telling about the next five years of piano lessons. This book is supposed to be a comedy, not a tragedy.

Years went by, and Mr. Jacobs passed away. This left Mrs. Jacobs all alone. For some reason, Mrs. Jacobs never ran her air conditioner, which made piano lessons in the summer months very unpleasant. I don't know if it was because of the cost or if it just made her too cold. Mrs. Jacobs would leave her windows open so a breeze could blow through, and some of her windows did not have screens on them.

One summer, a black tom cat showed up in the neighborhood. He was larger than most domestic cats, and his coat was the shiniest and silkiest I had ever seen. One day, he must have smelled Mrs. Jacobs' cooking and decided to investigate. She was standing in front of her stove thinking she was very much alone. As she continued cooking, the black cat decided to try to woo Mrs. Jacobs into giving him something to eat. Without a sound he jumped through an open window, snuck over to her, and rubbed his soft fur against her leg.

Mrs. Jacobs started screaming before she even saw what had touched her. The cat flew straight for the window and was gone before she could process what had just happened.

After this incident, the black cat started hanging out at our house. He was determined that we were going to adopt him, but my parents had different plans. We had been building a new house and were doing a lot of the work ourselves. We moved away from our old beloved neighborhood to our new home before we had sold our old house. No one was living at our old house except for the big black cat. Mrs. Jacobs started complaining to my parents. She wanted to know when we were going to come get "our cat." We kept denying ownership of that cat, but to her thinking he <u>was</u> ours. We heard rumors that he was causing trouble for the other neighbors, too, but I am not sure if those were not just fabricated stories to get us to remove the cat. Eventually we brought him to our new house and named him D.C. (Yes, we still were not overly clever.) We had gotten the name from the movie "That Darn Cat".

We already owned a cat named Wally. ("Wally" was short for Calico. I would have to go around the world with that story to explain how that nickname came about.) She was one of the greatest cats ever, but I won't go into all that either. Wally did lack some social skills, however. She got along great with people, but not with other animals. Now that D.C. was around, Wally was not a happy kitty. D.C. was bigger and definitely more street wise than Wally. These traits were very much to her disadvantage. However, she was a clever cat.

My family and I were all in the house one day when we heard Wally making horrible cries for help. Mom ran to the garage and found Wally crouching in a corner with D.C. ready to pounce on her. Mom told him what a "bad kitty" he was the entire time that she was chasing him with the broom. Don't worry. D.C. was always too fast to be caught by anyone wielding a broom.

These garage attacks occurred regularly and always ended with D.C. running for his life. We came to the conclusion that D.C. needed a new home.

Some time later, I was outside playing and saw D.C. walk into the garage. I knew Wally was in there, so I thought I had better make sure D.C. behaved himself. Neither of the cats saw me, because they were watching each other. Wally walked straight over to D.C. and started clawing at his face, hissing and growling all the while. Once she had gotten him sufficiently angry, she stopped slapping him and started making those horrible "help me" cries. Like a rocket, mom shot into the garage and heading straight for the broom. I stopped her and told her about Wally's naughty trick. We proceeded to tell Wally what a "bad kitty, bad kitty" she was. We decided to stop rescuing Wally from D.C. Wally, however, continued to attack D.C.

There came a day when D.C. had had enough. While in the backyard, Wally went over to him growling and slapping. D.C. took out after her, and Wally realized she was in trouble. She started running as fast as her fat little legs could carry her, but she was not fast enough. Not only did D.C. have a larger frame, he was all muscle. They were running across the yard when D.C. caught up with her. He slapped at Wally's back legs. Her back legs went flying into the air, and Wally did at least two or three somersaults. Her gymnastic form was so bad that it was hard to tell how many times she flipped. D.C. stopped and watched her tumble. He then walked away. His work was done.

Lesson Learned: If you cry wolf too many times, you better beware of black cats.

The Problem with Peas

There is one food I hate so badly that words really cannot describe my true dislike for it. This vegetable is green peas. Some people call them English peas. Some call them French peas, but I simply call them yuck!

My father, who believes in large helpings of food, insisted that I eat a helping of peas whenever we had them for supper. They really made me gag and worse. (Don't worry, I won't even go there.) How I felt did not affect my father's opinion at all. He still insisted that I eat them.

I finally came up with a plan. During supper, I would carefully scoop up a spoonful of peas and slide them under my plate. I would do this one spoonful at a time throughout supper. I had to be careful that no one saw me. Eventually my plate would start hiking up on one side. I would then casually put a hand on each side of my plate and push it down toward the table, rotating the plate slightly while pressing the peas flat.

After supper, I would wait for Pop to leave the table. I then would have to really work at unsticking the plate from the table. (Mashed peas are a good adhesive.) The next step was to carry my plate to the sink. I suppose I thought, like most children, that the plates magically cleaned themselves, and that no one would figure out my secret. As it turned out, Mom figured out the whole thing, but she never told Pop on me. I don't think she wanted to hear all the crying, wailing, and worse that would happen if I had to eat

those peas. After all everyone was happier this way:
Pop thought I was eating my peas. My brother
thought I was being forced to eat my peas. I was not
eating my peas. Well, maybe not everyone was
happy with the situation. Mom had to clean up the
peas. (If I were her, I would have marched my hinny
to the kitchen to scrape those plates.) Eventually
Mom stopped cooking green peas. I suppose she was
tired of living a lie.

Lesson Learned: Peas will always be yucky.

Creative Wardrobe Solutions

I have some creative relatives. On one occasion, one of my relatives, let's call her "Glad", was getting ready for work. Glad decided to get some meat out of her garage freezer. She was going to let the meat thaw all day, so she could cook it for supper that evening.

Glad went out into the garage and shut the door behind her. As soon as she heard the door shut, she realized she had locked herself out of the house. She was already running late for work, as usual. She started stressing about further irritating her employer.

The situation would not have been so bad if being locked out were her only problem. Her main problem was that she was wearing only her underwear. To further complicate things, she lived in the country, and there was a field between her house and her nearest neighbor's house. Glad is a sophisticated lady with an outstanding reputation in the community for her style and grace. Yet, here she was going to be late again with no dignified solution for her current situation. She started searching through the garage for things to wear and did what any clever lady would have done. She found a large black garbage bag. She tore a hole in it for her head and one for each arm. She donned her new dress and ran across the field, barefoot. The only neighbor who was home was the man of the house. She offered no explanation for her apparel but asked to use his phone. Glad used her one call to call her husband, and he showed up about thirty minutes later. He was surprised by her black plastic dress but did not ask for an explanation. After all, he had been married to her for many years and was accustomed to the sitcom-like situations in which his wife could find herself. As you would expect, Glad was REALLY late to work that day.

Lesson Learned: Plastic bags can be a versatile addition to your wardrobe.

Not so Clever of an Idea

I have always had a terrible sweet tooth and always tried to sneak treats out of the kitchen when I was growing up. Mom would be at the other end of the house, but she could always hear me getting into that Charles Chips cookie tin no matter how quiet I was.

One thing I usually could get away with was eating Kool Aid. Yes, I mean eating dry Kool Aid. It came in a canister and had a handy scoop inside. I would get a scoop full of Kool Aid, sneak out to the back yard, and eat it.

I never failed to get choked on that powder, because I was trying to eat it quickly before I got caught. No one ever caught me though, so I choked in solitude.

One day, I was staying at my Aunt Vesta and Uncle Chuck's house. They were busy doing things, and I found I was in desperate need of some sugar. On the kitchen table I found packets of sugar. How cool. I would not have to dirty a spoon and leave evidence (although I doubt the thought of cleaning up my messes and getting rid of evidence had ever occurred to me before this occasion).

I grabbed a couple of the pink packets and headed to the back yard. I ripped the packets open and emptied them both into my mouth. To my horror, I found out that those pink packets did not contain sugar. I started spitting and gagging. I tried scraping my tongue with my fingers, but I could not

get rid of that bitter taste. This was my first
encounter with Sweet and Low.

Lesson Learned: Before you sneak something to the
back yard, read the label.

Trouble on the Roof Top

When I was in second grade, one of my favorite television shows was *Little House on the Prairie*. This show inspired my best friend Carla and me to wear our granny dresses, so we would look like the Ingalls girls. We wore those dresses everywhere. My granny dress was made of boring shades of grey with big 70's flowers and shapes on it. The ankle length dress was rather straight, which was unlike Laura and Mary Ingalls' dresses.

My other favorite fashion accessory at this time was my pair of suede Indian moccasins. They had suede soles and ties like real moccasins.

It was the 1970's, so we only had three TV stations like everyone else. This was accepted by most as being just the way it was except by my father. Being a mechanical engineer, he loved new electronic gadgets. His newest gadget purchase was an antenna that could rotate. This allowed the television to get better reception and to receive more channels.

Every new gadget requires installation. This is where I came in. As usual, I was wearing my granny dress and moccasin combination when Pop came into the house one day. "I need your help." was his famous line that really meant "Come outside for hours of torturous boredom." As I followed him outside, I noticed the extension ladder leaning against the house. "Go up the ladder." Pop said." "Why?" I asked. "We're going to put up our new antenna." He replied. After I climbed a couple rungs, I asked,

"Should I change clothes?" "No," Pop replied, "that would take too long." As I continued up the ladder, I noticed that I was having a good bit of trouble with my long straight granny dress. Getting from the top of the ladder to the roof was a little scary in a dress, but I did not fall or die. Once on the roof, I quickly found that suede-soled Indian moccasins do not have much traction on a slanted, shingled roof.

Because my ankles were nearly tied together by the small opening at the hem of my dress, I had to be concerned even more with slipping and sliding. When one foot slid, the other foot quickly followed. I could take only little bitty steps, so I decided to move up the slanted roof on my hands and feet. This caused me to repeatedly step on the hem of my dress. When I tried to hold my dress up with one hand, I started sliding down the roof. I could certainly relate to the adage of "…taking one step forward and two steps back." My dad was so engrossed in his project that he apparently did not notice my struggle with the slanted roof and gravity's pull.

It took a while, but I finally made it to the top of the roof. By that time, I had come up with a plan. I would straddle the peak of the roof. If one foot slipped, I would press my other foot into the opposite side of the roof. Because my dress was so taut around my ankles, I did not have to worry about sliding down either side of the roof or doing the splits. I did have to worry, however, about my dress splitting up the sides because of all the pressure it was under. I do not know how many people in our neighborhood saw me on our roof, but I was trying to act like the whole situation was normal. It was just any ordinary day with me on the roof wearing my granny dress and Indian moccasins. Luckily, Pop was installing the new antenna right at the end of the roof's peak, so all I had to do was walk straight ahead.

Everything was going fine until we finished the installation and needed to dismount from the roof. First I had to turn around. After floundering around a bit, I ended up doing a "sit down, twirl around" move. I walked back to the other end of the house, straddling the peak. I thought that slipping and sliding my way up the roof was scary. Coming down was much worse. I believe the inspiration for snowboarding may have come from some experience similar to mine.

Pop was already at the top of the ladder. I aimed my body right for the ladder and him. Looking back, it is a wonder I did not push Pop and the ladder off the side of house. It would have been a long ride to the ground below for all of us. As I smacked into him, Pop exclaimed, "Quit horsing around!" Apparently he did not see the terror in my eyes.

Lesson Learned: Granny dresses and moccasins do not belong on the rooftop. Also, if you see my dad with a ladder, RUN.

Cookies are for Sharing?

One thing I have learned after spending a good bit of time with children is that they do not savor their food, especially sweets, like we grown-ups do. Apparently, my father had come to the same conclusion when I was growing up. I did not realize this until my teenage years. I remember looking into the cookie jar as a child and seeing those cheap tasteless cookies. You may know the kind. They were very thin and came about eleven dozen to a box. Sometimes I ate one, but usually I put the lid back on the cookie jar and raided the brown sugar jar or Kool Aid container instead.

It was not until I was in high school or college that I caught my father performing his treachery when he thought no one was looking. I watched him open the cookie jar. He gently and quietly laid the jar on its side. He then dug to the bottom of the cookie jar where he had hidden the good cookies. All those years, he had been hiding the good cookies at the bottom of the cookie jar and covering them with cheap cookies.

Lesson Learned: If you have something that is really good to eat, hide it from your children and your husband. Just remember that this does not always work. You may forget where you hid it, or your children may ask, "Where is the chocolate? I know you have some, because I can smell it on your breath!"

Clever Comebacks

My family has been going to the same church for longer than my lifetime. After my husband and I were married, we often sat on the same pew with my parents.

One Sunday my mom and my husband were sitting next to each other. The music minister invited everyone to stand to sing. Everyone stood except my husband. He just sat there with his head bowed and eyes closed. My mom nudged him and said, "Wake up. We are about to sing." Without raising his head, he gave my mom a sideways glance and said, "I was praying." My mom politely apologized and apologized. He kept his head lowered, but the grin on his lips told the real truth. I leaned around my husband and whispered to Mom, "He wasn't praying. He was sleeping." My husband's body started shaking from trying to contain his laughter. He never confessed his deception.

Lesson Learned: Do not sit next to my husband in church. You could be struck by a lightning bolt.

Chapter 4

Those Embarrassing Times

Dairy Queen Moments

Occasionally, Pop would give into his weakness for ice cream. He would get my brother and me to get off our dolly bobsled, and take us to the local Dairy Queen. While waiting for our order, I would often stand next to Pop with my arms wrapped around his leg, just above the knee. I don't know how old I was then, but hopefully I was pretty young. On one of these ice cream runs, we were waiting for our turn to order our frozen treat. I took my usual stand hugging onto Pop's leg. Apparently I was not paying attention to what was going on around me. For whatever reason, I looked up and saw that the man whose leg I was hugging was not my father. I looked up at him. He looked down at me. I started screaming, still holding tight to his leg.

The poor man looked around at everyone else as if to say, "What do I do!" He put his hands up in the air to show that he was not touching me. I continued to hold on and scream.

My father is easily embarrassed. I think he tried acting like he did not know whose child I was, but finally, without moving from his place in line he said, "Karen, let go of him and GET over here!" He added a quick and irritated "come here" gesture with his hand.

I let go of the man and carefully backed away from him, just in case he was going to grab me. The next couple of minutes were very awkward. No one said anything, and everyone avoided eye contact. Everyone, except for my brother, that is. Jerry reminded me that I was an embarrassment to the family.

Lesson Learned: Be careful whose leg you grab.

Awful Moments

Parents can make unwise decisions sometimes. I personally think giving a boy a BB gun falls into that category. Giving a girl a BB gun is probably not really a great idea, either.

Pop gave Jerry a BB gun when we were kids. (I'm pretty sure it was against my mom's wishes.) My dad had bought some land outside of town, and he thought our land in the country would be the perfect place for target practice.

One day Pop and Jerry went out to the property. My brother took his new BB gun along to amuse himself. While holding the gun, somehow it "mysteriously" went off. The tiny BB hit the back window of Pop's 1967 Chevrolet truck. (It was the cutest little window, much smaller than truck windows of today.) As Jerry stood in shock looking at the new hole near the corner of the window, a small crack began creeping its way out of the tiny, tiny BB hole. The crack quickly traveled from one corner of the window to another. My brother jumped into the bed of the truck and put his hands at the end of the crack to try to keep it from spreading. Then another crack started from the hole, and another crack, and another. By now my brother was crying like a school girl who just lost the role of princess in the school play.

After all the cracking had stopped, the window looked like someone had etched an elaborate road map into it. All the roads led to that one little hole in the top left corner.

I thought a miracle had happened when I saw the truck window and heard the story. For once my brother actually got caught doing something, and I was nowhere around to catch any blame. I knew he would be punished. Was he? No. Pop felt it was obvious that Jerry regretted what he had done by the way he sobbed.

Later as my brother relayed the story to me, I could tell he was still visibly upset. I played the role of the perfect consoling sister and said, "Wow, you shot out the window of Pop's truck. You know how much he loves that truck. He's probably really sad. It's such an old truck. He probably won't be able to get a new window for it." I think that was about the time he hit me. (Anger management classes were not offered back then.)

Lesson Learned: My brother always gets out of trouble. He can, however, cry like a girl when the circumstances are right.

Hotels and Tattoos

When I was younger, my family did a lot of traveling. It was always in our groovy '69 Pontiac Catalina. The car was hunter green when hunter green was not cool, and this car will forever be referred to as The Bomb.

In later years my parents taught my brother and me humility by making us drive The Bomb to school. It was a good idea now that I look back on it. It was so huge that we were much more likely to survive a crash. It wasn't cool, so we did not have crowds of kids wanting to ride with us and goading us into trouble. It was such a tank that if you had a minor fender bender, it did not show. (Don't ask me how I know. Don't ask my brother, either.) Finally, if you had friends who also had tanks for transportation, you could bump their bumpers just to say "hello", and neither car was hurt.

In The Bomb, my family traveled from Tennessee to California in a zigzag pattern in order to see various relatives and sights along the way. When traveling, we never made hotel reservations ahead of time. When we came to a desired town, we would drive from hotel to hotel looking for one with a swimming pool, a diving board, and a slide. These three amenities were a must. Finding a pool with a slide was usually a problem. Unfortunately, finding a hotel with vacancies that met our pool requirements became an ever bigger problem. Sometimes we had to settle for just a pool and diving board.

While traveling in the car, my parents always separated my brother and me. This meant one parent was in the back seat with one child at all times. Mom and Pop took turns driving. Jerry and I couldn't wait for Mom to drive, scary as that always is, because Pop would sleep. Pop is an unbelievably sound sleeper. While he slept, whichever child was in the back seat with him drew pictures on his arms and ear lobes with ballpoint pens. He ended up with the most elaborate tattoos that a seven or a ten year old could draw.

Seeing our conservative dad with tattoos was hilarious, and he didn't complain about them. The best part about Pop's tattoos was when he had to go into a hotel to make reservations. He would go up to the front desk with his tattoo-clad arms and drawn-on earrings and ask for a room. He always acted as if there was nothing wrong with his body art no matter how the clerk reacted.

Lesson Learned: To keep your mild-mannered dad out of trouble, do not give him a tattoo that reads "Killer" or "Make Me".

Water on the Phone Lines

I have not really written that much about Aunt Vesta's husband, Uncle Chuck. He was a lot of fun, and he loved pulling pranks on people. There was one he pulled that is my favorite. I think I like it so much because it was so dumb.

Uncle Chuck decided to pull a prank on the wife of one of his good friends. First he called her and disguised his voice. He told her that he worked with the phone company and that the company was having trouble with water on the lines and needed her help.

Being the helpful sort, the wife gladly agreed. Uncle Chuck - I mean, the telephone man - warned her that she would be unable to use her phone all day. He pleaded that they really needed her help despite the inconvenience. The wife still agreed. All the good lady would have to do, after she hung up the phone, was to put the phone receiver in a big cooking pot. She needed to use the biggest pot she had. The phone company would then blow the water off the lines, through the phone cord and into the cooking pot. The telephone man told her that she would need to check the pot from time to time and to empty out the water every so often so the pot would not overflow.

After hanging up the phone, the wife stretched the phone cord across the kitchen, put the biggest pot she had on the kitchen table, placed the receiver in the pot, and went about her housework.

A little while later, the wife's husband came home. He noticed the phone cord stretched across the room and the receiver lying in the pot and asked his wife what was going on. She explained what the phone company had asked her to do. She went on to say that she was catching the water that the phone company was blowing off the lines. The husband said, "Please don't tell me you fell for that!" His wife insisted that she was helping the phone company and that "This is all very logical."

Against her wishes, the husband removed the receiver from the empty pot and gave Uncle Chuck a call. I don't know if Uncle Chuck was the first suspect or not. When Uncle Chuck received the call, neither man could contain his laughter. The wife, however, did not find it funny and never quite forgave Uncle Chuck. The fact that her husband would never let her live it down probably did not help.

Lesson Learned: Every adolescent needs a master prankster like Uncle Chuck to teach them the art of good, clean, pranks.

Sock Fights

When I was in sixth grade, gaucho pants became popular. I loved them. Wearing them made me feel like Barbara Stanwyck in *Big Valley*. All I needed was a horse and Lee Majors. Another fashion must at that time was gaucho socks, a type of thin trouser knee sock with designs on them. Mine were sky blue, imprinted with an artistic rendition of a turn-of-the-century woman dressed in white.

I loved those socks. I loved wearing socks in general. In fact, I loved sleeping in my socks, because they kept my feeties warm. My Pop had issues with me wearing socks to bed. He was opposed to this habit, because he believed that your feet were supposed to breathe while you slept. (Apparently your feet do not need to breathe during waking hours.)

I sometimes sleep with my eyes open. I know that sounds creepy and seems totally off the subject, but it really is relevant to this story. While I am sleeping wide-eyed, I sometimes work what is going on around me into my dreams.

I frequently watched *Gilligan's Island* reruns, and I must have recently seen one of the episodes with wild headhunters in it. Somehow Pop found out that I had worn my tight polyester gaucho socks to bed one night, and decided that he was going to perform a sock "intervention". He came into my bedroom. Without saying a word, he pulled back the sheet and grabbed each of my feet. He obviously knew nothing about removing polyester gaucho socks because he grabbed the fabric at my toes and started pulling. This made those tight socks hold on tighter.

On this particular night, I was sleeping with my eyes open. Instead of seeing my dad, I saw/dreamed a headhunter grabbing my feet! I started kicking. Pop kept pulling at those socks. I kept kicking. Pop would not give up. By the time he got my socks off, those things were stretched to about five feet long. Amazingly I did not wake up. It was not until the next morning when Pop was complaining about the terrible time he had getting my socks off that I realized that he was the headhunter in my dream. He then fussed at me for putting up such a fight.

The sock removal incident was so unpleasant that Pop never attempted it again.

Lesson Learned: If you see a headhunter in your bedroom, do not put up a fight. Just give him your socks.

Funeral Visits

There was a family in our town that loved going to funeral visitations, and they did not need to know the deceased person to attend.

This hobby of theirs may seem a little odd, but their presence was always sure to liven up any visitation, and the grandmother of the family was the star attraction.

The family would enter the funeral home and chat with others who had come to pay their last respects. Gradually these funeral chasers would make it up to the family members of the deceased who were standing near the casket. They would give their condolences. Then the grandmother would walk over to the casket and look at the deceased, let out a wail, and faint. She did this at almost every visitation. We kids loved it. Several of the men enjoyed it, too. There were quite a few people, however, who were not amused, but like it or not, when the funeral chasing grandmother walked into a funeral home, most eyes were on her.

She had gained such a reputation that eventually one or two men began to follow behind her as soon as she headed toward the coffin. The men would get into position, and would catch her as she started to "faint" and pull her to another room with her feet dragging behind them. They would lay her on a couch and leave her to "recover". There was always some newcomer, though, who did not know the drill. The newcomer would be astonished at how no one seemed to care about this elderly woman's health. The newcomer would then make a big fuss over grandmother, thus encouraging her disruptive behavior and guaranteeing an encore performance at the next visitation.

No matter how you felt about grandmother's behavior, she could always get your mind off your troubles.

Lesson Learned: If you are going to faint, have an entourage with you to catch you and keep you from hurting yourself. The entourage also gives your "faint" a little more flare.

Dating in Stolen Cars

When I was growing up, one of my favorite neighbors was an elderly widow named Miss Edith. Miss Edith had a lot of spunk and was always full of surprises. Even in her eighties, her eyesight was amazing. For instance, she could spot a four-leaf clover in a clover patch. She was always pressing those four-leaf clovers and giving them to the people she liked. No, not everyone got a four leaf clover from Miss Edith.

When you paid Miss Edith a visit, you had better plan on having a cup of coffee. To decline a cup of coffee was considered a great insult. Miss Edith made the strongest coffee I ever drank. After a visit, my eyelids would twitch for the rest of the day from the enormous amount of caffeine I had consumed. I finally wised up and started asking for a Coke instead of coffee. As it turned out, apparently all that mattered was that Miss Edith's guests were drinking a cup of something. As a hostess, she felt she had failed if her guests' thirsts were not quenched. My eyelids were relieved.

Miss Edith had no children and little family left, so she would tell my mom and me her funny life-stories. One of my favorites was a dating story. There was a young man who had been trying to talk Miss Edith into going on a date with him. She kept declining his offers, but finally she reluctantly agreed.

On the day of the date, the young man unwisely started drinking very early in the day and was quite drunk by the time he was supposed to pick up Miss Edith. He was at a bar in town, and was so drunk that he could not find his car. Again, he made an unwise choice and decided to steal a ride.

When the young man showed up in Miss Edith's driveway, he was driving a school bus. Apparently that was all he could manage to steal. When Miss Edith's father saw the bus drive up, he stopped Miss Edith from going out of the house. He went out instead and greeted the young suitor. Miss Edith's father informed the young man that he did not allow his daughter to be picked up for a date in a school bus. After talking with the young man, Miss Edith's father also added that he did not allow his daughter to date a drunken man. With that he made the drunken man leave.

Miss Edith did not know what the young man did with the school bus. I have always wondered if he returned the bus, or if he got caught. After all, a drunk driving a stolen, yellow school bus should not be too hard to spot.

Lesson Learned: If your date drives up in a yellow school bus and can't walk a straight line, the date isn't going to go well.

Nursing Home Thieves

When I was in my early teen years, I would often go with my mom to visit a friend of the family at a local nursing home. It was on one such visit that I had a rather embarrassing scare.

For some reason, my mom and I had gotten separated. As I was walking down the hallway, I heard one of the patients calling for help from her room.

I looked around and saw no nurses or aides, so I went into the room. The patient was lying in her bed in no obvious distress. I asked her what was wrong. She asked me to come closer. The music from "Psycho" was sounding in my head, but I was young and naive and chose to ignore it.

When I got closer, the woman grabbed my arm with the fiercest grip and started yelling, "That's my watch! She stole my watch!" Ironically, it was Aunt Louise's watch that she had let me wear. This meant I couldn't really even say the watch was mine.

As two nurses came running into the room, I thought, "Great, I am going to be labeled as a nursing home thief, and they are going to take Aunt Louise's watch." I proclaimed my innocence as the woman told the nurses her story. One nurse turned to me and said, "Don't worry. She does this all the time."

Lesson learned: Wear only ugly jewelry to nursing homes. If someone there claims it, you will be glad to let it go.

Marrying Frank

When I was attending college at the University of Tennessee, occasionally I would go to nearby Jefferson City with my roommate, Lisa, to visit her family. Lisa's Uncle Frank still lived with his mother, who was Lisa's MaMaw, so we would see Uncle Frank when we visited MaMaw.

Uncle Frank was a character. On one visit, a painter stopped by the house. He was going to do some painting for MaMaw. MaMaw had stepped out of the room, and the painter wrongfully assumed that he could talk about the painting particulars with Uncle Frank. As the painter was trying to talk business, Uncle Frank started pointing out Lisa and me to the painter. The painter politely nodded to us then resumed talking business. Uncle Frank then pointed at me and said, "How do you like my new wife?" The painter looked at me in surprise. I tried not to look surprised myself and tried to play along. As the painter looked at me, Uncle Frank loudly exclaimed, "What are you doing looking at my wife?! She's my wife and you can't have her!" As Uncle Frank continued with his monologue, the poor painter realized he was fighting a losing battle. He verbally and physically back peddled all the way out the front door.

Lesson Learned: I felt like a runaway bride when I left MaMaw's. Boy, that felt good!

Bedroom Quandaries

My first few months of college at the University of Tennessee were lonely, and I was homesick. Coming home was something I looked forward to. My family isn't the mushy type, so I guess I had to show my parents how I missed them in ways other than affection.

One weekend while my parents were out of the house, I short sheeted their bed. The next morning, Mom cornered me. "You short sheeted the bed, didn't you?!" she demanded. I confessed. She said, "There is only one way for you not to get in trouble over this." I listened intently while she explained. She had gone to bed first the night before and was the only victim of my prank. She did not tell my father about my deed. In order for me to get out of trouble, I would have to short sheet the bed again, but make sure that my dad was the recipient of the prank. For a moment I was concerned. Was I falling into a continuous stream of blackmailing threats? Then I realized that if things got too bad, I could just rat on Mom, so I agreed to the plan.

That night, I once again short sheeted my parents' bed. I alerted Mom, so when she got in bed first; she just lay on top of the sheets. Eventually, Pop came to bed. Mom pretended to be asleep and successfully contained her laughter. Pop tried to get in bed. He got back out of bed. Pop tried to get in bed again. He grumbled and got back out. He pulled back the sheets and blankets trying to figure out what he was doing wrong. After all, Mom was able to get in bed. By now, he was really grumbling. He "woke" Mom and said, "Something is wrong with our sheets. I think someone short sheeted them." For some reason his thoughts went straight to me. "Karen did this!" he declared. "I'm going to wake her up right now and make her fix this!"

Mom was able to calm Pop down and talked him into not waking me. By morning, Pop had calmed down a lot. My only punishment was being fussed at and occasionally glared at.

Lesson Learned: Affection can be shown in many ways.

Undershirt Obstacles

I continued to feel the need to show my parents how much I missed them when I was at college. I decided that I needed to do something to make my parents think of me while I was away.

I had observed something about some men that gave me an idea. Have you ever noticed how guys put on their t-shirts? First they put their arms in each sleeve. Then they pull the shirt over their head. With this in mind, I snuck three or four of my dad's undershirts out of his drawer. I then sewed up the neck hole of each of these shirts. I neatly shuffled them in with his other t-shirts so they would not be all stacked together.

I could imagine Pop getting ready for work early one morning and wondering why his head couldn't find the neck hole. Since he is an engineer, I imagined this could be a type of mind puzzle exercise. One nice aspect of this prank was that it was the prank that kept on giving, since there was more than one altered shirt in Pop's drawer.

Sadly, I never heard anything from Pop about what he found in his undershirt drawer. He never said a word about it. He had Mom do it for him. Instead of my parents now missing me, I believe they felt safer that I was away.

I have discovered different variations of this prank, and have tested them on my husband. That is all I should say about that.

Lesson Learned: Be very choosy whose underwear you alter.

New Dishes

My Aunt Louise had moved to California when I was a child. As I got older, I started visiting her during my summer breaks from school. During my freshman year of college, Aunt Louise got remarried. The plan was for me to go to California during my summer break and meet my new uncle.

My new Uncle Don had decided to cook supper for us, all by himself, to celebrate my arrival. I got the impression this did not happen often, and that I should feel honored. I was.

Uncle Don started telling me about the menu for the evening. He said, "I am going to fix you a Mexican dish tonight. It is called "tacos"." Apparently he thought since I was from Tennessee, I was too backward to know what a taco was. This was that once in a lifetime opportunity to act as if I were Sandra Dee in one of those Tammy movies. I asked, "Tocooo? What's a tocooo?" My uncle then tried to help me with my pronunciation of the word. He wasn't even going to tell me what a taco was until I could pronounce it correctly. He kept trying to help me pronounce it, but it was just too hard for this Tennessee girl to grasp. He would say, "It is pronounced "taco"." I would repeat, "Tocooo?" "No", he would repeat, "ta-co". He pronounced the word over and over again, each time a little more slowly and in a more irritated voice.

Finally Aunt Louise couldn't take it anymore. "You nut! She knows what a taco is. She's eaten them all her life." Uncle Don looked at me questioningly. I laughed. He left the room. Aunt Louise and I had to finish cooking our Mexican dish ourselves.

Lesson Learned: When traveling out of the South, I think it would be fun to bring a goat and tell everyone my name is Tammy. I would then pretend everything is new and amazing to me. I think it could be great fun. The down side would be that I would have to clean up after that goat.

Bad Signals

During my teenage years, my family decided to go on vacation with another family to Gatlinburg, TN. We had gotten to town earlier than expected and stopped by the Chamber of Commerce to pick up a bunch of brochures and start planning the fun things that we could do while we were there.

The Chamber was on the opposite side of the street from us, so my dad said he would let my mom and me out. As usual there was no plan on how to meet back up. Mom and I got out of the car and crossed the street. We gathered brochures and left the building. Pop had driven the car a little farther up the road but was in the farthest lane from us. When he saw us, he pointed to us, then pointed to the sidewalk on his side of the street, and finally twirled his finger in a circular motion. Mom and I interpreted this to mean, "Cross the street, and I will stop to let you in the car."

After we finally got across the street, we noticed that Pop had kept driving. We figured he did not want to slow down traffic by stopping, so we would have to jog or run to catch up with him. To Mom and me, walking quickly is the equivalent to jogging or running because that is pretty much as fast as we move. Before we knew it, the car was out of sight.

We continued walking for about an hour and then sat on a short brick wall and waited for the next hour. When Pop finally drove up, he was madder than an old wet hen, but guess what? Mom and I were pretty hot ourselves.

Evidently, when Pop pointed to Mom and me, pointed to the sidewalk, and twirled his finger, we were supposed to translate that to mean, "You two cross the street. Wait for me right there, and I am going to drive around the block and pick you up on my way back around." He had been circling that block for two hours. Meanwhile, Mom and I had walked well past that first block.

Lesson Learned: Add to my "to do" list: teach Pop sign language.

Room Key Complications

This story still makes me shudder, but I will tell it anyway.

I had recently graduated from college and had gotten my first full-time job. A co-worker, Charlotte, and I drove to Decatur, AL on a business trip. After we got to our hotel, we went up to our room. We had taken only a few things up with us, so I told Charlotte I would get the rest of our luggage from the car. She left our hotel door slightly open, so I would not have to mess with a key and luggage.

I went to the car, and tucked a bag under each arm. I then grabbed a suitcase with each hand (Neither of us travel light). I made it up the elevator successfully and walked down the hallway. I came to our door and pushed it open with my foot, took a couple steps into the room and set down the suitcases and bags. As I stood up, my eyes met with a man who was lying on the bed. This man was extremely rotund and wearing only his underwear.

I was shocked and rather confused at the sight of this man. He seemed even more shocked than I. He frantically said, "You're in the wrong room! You're in the wrong room!" I repeatedly said, "I'm sorry." while trying not to look up at him.

I tried so hard to gather up my things, but he had me so shaken that I could not manage to gather everything up in my arms. By this time, he had leaped off the bed and was jumping up and down while telling me, "You're in the wrong room! You're in the wrong room! Get out!"

"Oh, please," I begged, "don't get up." (Really, please don't get up, because I am seeing more than I want to already!) I picked up the suitcases, but then I could not pick up the smaller bags. Then I picked up the smaller bags, but would drop one as soon as I grabbed a suitcase. I really did feel like I was living out a scene from an episode of the "Lucy Show."

The man must have been afraid his wife would walk in and find me in their room, or maybe he thought I was going to take advantage of him. I am guessing his wife was carrying all their luggage by herself from the car. I wondered if she would end up in our room with Charlotte.

I finally was able to gather up all our bags and apologize once more as I hurried out the door. Luckily I did not run into any wife as I fled to my room.

Lesson Learned: Paying attention to hotel room numbers is very important.

Hot Cherry Pie

Pop's mom, Granny, was one tough old bird. She was only 4'11" tall, but nobody wanted to mess with her. We did not realize it at the time but, while in her late seventies, Granny had been having a series of mini strokes. The strokes had started to affect her judgment and memory.

One day near her home in Pennsylvania, Granny caused a car wreck. She was totally unaware of it, so she drove away. The owners of the other two cars involved in the crash got her tag number and called the police. Two officers showed up at Granny's door and left with her driver's license. Granny gave them a few (or maybe several) unpleasant words as they left.

The family was relieved that Granny was no longer allowed to drive. We were even more relieved that those officers were the ones who had to tell her to stay off the road. From the way she ranted about the police and by the things she claimed to have said to them, those officers more than earned their pay that day.

Granny also had trouble getting along with her neighbors. I do not know if her anger toward them was justifiable or not, but she was always threatening to sell her house and move away from those neighbors. One day, without warning, she did sell her house. She did not get that great of a price for the house and now she had nowhere to live.

Granny was the mother of eight children. Because she could be rather difficult to deal with, her children decided to take turns keeping her. Each of her children would keep Granny for two weeks at a time then pass her on to the next sibling. The plan was to continue doing this until a more permanent living arrangement was worked out for her. Granny's children were rather spread out across the United States, so Granny became quite the traveler. When it was my dad's turn, my parents had Granny flown to Nashville, and we picked her up at the airport.

I was able to spend a good bit of time with Granny during this visit. I noticed that she was telling me a lot of stories that I had never heard before. Some of them were amazing, but I did not question their accuracy.

One evening during Granny's stay, Mom invited a few of her family members over to have dinner and visit with Granny. Doyle and I could not come, but I cannot remember why. Mom had put a Mrs. Smith's cherry pie in the oven. After dinner, Mom asked, "Who would like some hot cherry pie?" Granny exclaimed, "Hot cherry pie? Are you trying to kill us?!" Mom asked Granny what she was so upset about. Granny continued, "Don't you know that hot cherry pie is poisonous? Everybody knows that!"

I believe this is where Pop broke in in an attempt to keep Granny from insulting Mom any further. (It did not work, by the way.) Pop asked Granny what she was talking about, and Granny replied with a story that no one had heard before.

She had been to a dinner party years before at which hot cherry pie was served. A guest ate a piece and died before the evening was through. Of course, the pie was to blame. When Pop was later telling me the story, he said, "What a crazy story. Mum has never been to a formal dinner party in her life!" (As if that was the craziest part of that story.)

The next night, Doyle and I went to my parents' house for dinner. Aunt Louise and Uncle Don were there as well. The two of them had witnessed the ranting's of Granny the night before. No one brought up the topic of the previous night's dinner, but Doyle and I had secretly heard all about it. After dinner, my mom asked if anyone wanted dessert. Doyle perked right up and exclaimed, "I want some of that hot cherry pie!"

Uncle Don almost choked on his food. The eyes of Aunt Louise and Pop grew wide just before they looked down at their plates to avoid eye contact with anyone. They were expecting the volcano to blow. To our surprise, Granny just rolled her eyes and said nothing.

Lesson Learned: From that day on, I have threatened to feed Doyle hot cherry pie whenever he misbehaves.

Singing on the Floor

I had sung in my church choir and in ensembles for years, but I did not sing solos.

One day our choir director's secretary, Julie, a good friend of mine, told me, "The date for your solo had to be changed." "What solo?" I asked. She said, "The note's in your choir box." I stood there in confusion still asking, "What solo?" The rest of the day was a blur. All I could think about was coming up with a rational excuse to get out of this situation. Should I skip the country?

I started thinking about my children. My oldest hated to sing in children's choir. So that she would be less anxious, I would ask her teachers to let her stand on the back row. I was told more than once that, "A parent has never before asked me to have their child hidden on the back row behind the other children." My younger child did fine singing with groups, but you could forget about getting her to sing a solo.

I came to the conclusion that if I were going to help my children overcome their fears, I was going to have to face my own. My girls were right there with me cheering me on, too.

The night of my solo arrived. I made it through my first solo with several friends singing backup for me. Having my friends there cheering me on helped me through the song. The congregation could not see my children in the balcony making faces at me. My girls thought they were helping.

Apparently it helped keep a smile on my friend's faces.

A few months later, I was scheduled to sing another solo. As the night of the event grew closer, I began to stress over what to wear. Mainly I stressed over what shoes to wear, because I did not want to fall down in front of everyone.

The night came and I showed up early enough to practice with the band. Another group was already singing, so I decided to sneak my lyric cheat sheet to the fold back speakers on stage.

I went up three steps, crouched down to place the sheet on the speaker, and backed down two steps. But, I forgot about the third step. Because I was still crouched over, I rolled like a roly-poly bug from the base of my spine to the top of my neck. Both my feet went flying into the air. Of course I was wearing a somewhat short, straight dress. Luckily this helped to keep my legs from spreading, but it is possible that my undies made a quick and shocking appearance. I immediately hopped up, hoping that no one would notice, and tried to casually walk away. Luckily, a sweet man, Dick, was nearby and helped me up. I think he helped block most everyone's ability to see me hobble away. The fall had been a little rough on my ankle.

This mishap only added to my nervousness, but I made it through the solo. After the church service was over, two different friends separately came up to me and asked, "What were you doing before church? Why were you rolling around in the floor?" and "Did you fall or were you just fooling around?" I replied, "Who am I, Carol Burnett? I fell!"

Lesson Learned: I don't have to worry about what shoes to wear when singing a solo. I can look like an idiot in any kind of footwear.

Chapter 5
More Animal Predicaments

Trying to Kill a Mockingbird

When I was a teenager, we moved out into the country. This allowed us more room to have pets. Of course there were other animals that were also around. These animals were of the wildlife variety. Being one with nature is not always a good thing. Our pets found this out when a mockingbird built her nest in one of our tall oak trees. There was no way any of our cats could reach that nest, but that did not stop the mockingbird from insuring her babies' safety. She would let out with these terrible war cries. The dive bombing would then start. She would aim for the hind ends of our dog or one of our cats, swoop down, peck the animal with her beak, and then climb back up into the sky. Our pampered pets were horrified.

We could hear the mockingbird's cries from inside the house. I would run outside and yell at it. I tried throwing acorns at it, but nothing deterred that bird from pecking our pets. One day when Mom and I were in the house, we heard the war cries. My mom had had enough of that bird! She stopped me from running outside and said she was going to "handle it". My non-violent mother then got her pistol and headed outside.

The mockingbird was perched on our wooden shed. Mom fired the first shot and missed. She moved the barrel of the gun slightly to the right and fired. She missed again. She moved the barrel slightly back to the left and fired. She missed again. This went on and on. The bird did not even move. She probably figured out she was safer staying in the same spot.

One of our neighbors came over to see what all the shooting was about. Mom pointed to the bird and explained the situation. The neighbor went back to his house and returned with a shotgun. You do not have to aim too accurately when you shoot a small bird with birdshot as it turns out.

Lesson Learned: Sometimes you really do have to kill a mockingbird.

Nervous Times

When I was growing up, we had a good family friend with a nervous problem. Maybe a nervous condition would be a better term. We all tried hard not to upset her. Don't get me wrong, she did not get mad or anything like that when something went wrong. In fact, she had the opposite problem. She would withdraw completely from everyone and everything. She was having just such a reclusive spell one time, and we had been trying to get her out of her house to come over to our house for dinner. Finally she agreed to come.

We were having a nice visit and everyone was seated at the table. My parents' kitchen and dining area are open, so you can see the kitchen from the dinner table. I had gone into the kitchen to get some forgotten dishes, when across the back ledge of the counter ran a little field mouse. I screamed.

Everyone asked "What's wrong?!" I knew if I said there was a mouse in the house, our nervous guest might not deal with it very well, so I replied, "Nothing." (Great comeback, Karen. As if people just go around screaming when the urge hits them.)

Everyone looked at me funny, but amazingly they dropped the subject. We ate dinner, and everything was going fine. My mom decided we needed more rolls. I immediately jumped up and said, "Oh, let me get them." I'm sure my mom was thinking, "Since when is my teenage daughter so helpful?" Amazingly, she sat back down and did not question my behavior.

I pretended to walk happily to the kitchen, but as I went into the kitchen my steps slowed down. I was cautiously observing my surroundings the way Inspector Clouseau always looked for Cato to attack. I knew that mouse was still in the kitchen, but I did not see it. I did spot the bowl of yummy spoon rolls that mom had made, and I went straight for the bowl, which had a wide rim. As I lifted the bowl, I saw the mouse hiding under the rim of the roll bowl, and I almost touched the little guy. Once again the mouse darted away like a long grey blur. Once again I screamed. (Mice wouldn't bother me so much if they weren't so darn fast. If they could just slow down, I could make sure I was out of their way.) Once again everyone asked, "What is wrong?" My brother even asked, "What is wrong with you?" Once again I cheerfully answered, "Nothing."

I tried to think up an excuse like, "I occasionally have these screaming fits that I cannot control." but I knew Mom would just argue with me about it in front of everyone. Or instead of arguing, I was afraid Mom would ask questions like, "When is the first time this happened? How often do you randomly scream? Why have you not told me about this? Why are you shutting me out? I don't even know you anymore!" I really did not want to go there, so I kept my answer at "Nothing" and offered no explanation.

I was getting strange looks from everyone at the table now. The looks were the ones that say "What are you doing?" and, "Knock it off!" I was pretty quiet for the rest of the meal. When dinner was over, I suggested postponing clearing the table until later.

Once our guest had left, the family cornered me. I think they were ready to get out the tranquilizer gun and do some target practicing. When I told them there was a mouse in the kitchen, Mom high-stepped out of the room, looking everywhere she stepped. It would probably have been better to tell Mom about the kitchen mouse when we were somewhere other than the kitchen. As Mom did her tippy-toe, marching, scared dance around the house, I could hear her proclaim and occasionally squeal about how glad she was that our friend did not know about the mouse. Watching Mom do that weird dance helped me not feel like such an idiot for screaming.

When we caught the mouse, we turned it loose in our field. One of the cats then more than likely caught it again and brought it back to the house. Then the cat probably lost the mouse in the garage again. The mouse would then make it back into the house. Those good-for-nothing city cats were always catching mice, but they never knew what to do with them.

Lesson Learned: If you want to see a woman dance, just yell "Mouse!"

Dogs Really Will Eat Anything

One of my college roommates, Lisa, has an amazingly quick wit. She always has a great comeback, but she has a way of making her comebacks never come across as being too insulting.

One evening, she was walking through the apartment complex when she came upon a man walking his dog. She commented on what a cute dog the man had. The man was incensed that Lisa did not appear to know what type of dog he owned. "This is a shar-pei. He cost $1000." the man said. As he talked on and on about his wonderful and rare breed of dog, the shar-pei found the poop of some other dog and proudly ate his amazing discovery. The owner did not notice what his dog was doing, but Lisa did. She pointed to the dog and said, "Oh look, that rare dog cost $1000, yet he eats poop just like a mutt." The guy was shocked at his dog's behavior and at Lisa's lack of praise for his pooch. He quickly rushed "Wrinkles" home.

Lesson Learned: Don't brag about the superiority of your dog when he is near poop.

A Stinky Situation

I went on a lady's church retreat one weekend and was rooming with one of my girlfriends, Renee. We got ready for bed, but were having a hard time tolerating how warm our cabin was. When Renee opened the front door and let in some cool air, the wind blew her hair and gown back in a dramatic and picturesque way. She looked like someone out of a painting. Suddenly Renee jerked her head down and almost doubled over. She let out with an "OH!" and quickly fumbled to shut the door. She was not quick enough, though. The cabin filled with the horrible smell of a skunk's spray. Wouldn't you know, just as Renee opened the door, a skunk stopped at our door and sprayed?

Lesson Learned: Skunks can always find me.

My Secret Box

One thing I try to make sure I have in my life is laughter. There are many ways to achieve this, but some days are just too blue to be funny. Those are the days that I pull out my secret box, which contains hundreds of frozen moments in time, moments that can soften the hardest of days. My secret box is full of pictures, but these are not just any old pictures. Every one of these pictures has one or more flaws. Someone's head is chopped off. Someone has their eyes closed. Someone has their mouth full. However, my favorite "messed up" pictures are the ones where someone looks mad. I get out my "thought bubble" stickers I found at a scrapbooking store one time. I then make up what the person in the picture is thinking or saying. What I make up usually has nothing to do with what was going on when the picture was taken. The more the remarks are out of character for the photographed person, the better. Pictures of sweet and kind relatives are the best for this type of project. For example, having sweet grandma threatening to "take someone down" can be a lot of fun. After I alter enough pictures to lift my spirits, I put away my secret box, and no one has to know what I pretended they said.

You might think keeping a box of "messed up" pictures is depressing. The solution for this is easy: I throw away bad pictures of **myself.** I am certainly not going to hang on to pictures that can be used against me. Also, seeing a picture of myself looking like Two Ton Tessy is only going to ruin my day.

Lesson Learned: Don't show your secret box to friends or family members because their pictures will probably be in there.

Part II

If you do not have enough humor in your life, there is one sure cure: have children. Even if they do not do something to amuse you at one particular moment in time, your children are bound do something that everyone else around you will find amusing. Yes, you will be humiliated publicly from time to time. That is unavoidably part of being a parent.

I decided that this book needs to be written in two parts: lessons I learned before becoming a parent, and lessons I learned after becoming a parent. Although the Part Two phase of my life has been a much shorter phase, being a parent has taught me lessons at a much faster rate.

In case you are wondering, I am not going to write about my most humiliating parenting moments, because I do not want my children to sue me when they are grown. You do not have to worry, though. That still leaves hundreds of perfectly humiliating stories to share.

Chapter 6

Parenting Problems in the South

It's all in a Name

Many families have traditions that dictate what future generations will be named. My husband's family has one such tradition. I was informed that if I had a son, his middle name had to be Taylor. This was the middle name of every boy born in my husband's family for generations. No one knew why, but apparently that was not important. Doyle's Grandma Veazey said that she was not sure, but she thought Taylor was the name of the long ago doctor who delivered one of Doyle's ancestors. The tradition also dictated that my son's first name had to start with an "E". This would continue the family tradition of having the next generation's first name start with the next letter of the alphabet.

As the due date neared for my first child, I was asked what my child's name would be. I am sure some of the inquiries were to see if I were going to comply with the family tradition. I had thought long and hard about my answer. I finally replied, "If the baby is a boy, his name will be Elvis Taylor. If the baby is a girl, her name will be Graceland." I offered no hint as to whether I was serious or not. Doyle's family probably thought I was some kind of rebellious lunatic.

Doyle initially was horrified. "No son of mine is going to be named Elvis!" he said. "It's the only name that starts with an "E" that I will agree to." I replied. I think he was beginning to realize that my rebellious nature was not going to allow anyone to tell me what I was going to name the baby that I had been carrying around in my womb.

Luckily, God handled the dispute. Our first child was a daughter. To double my delight, our second child was also a daughter. I think the family was relieved that they did not have an Elvis in the family. After all, there really is only one Elvis. Ironically my oldest daughter's middle name does start with an "E". My nickname for her is Elvis. My youngest daughter's middle name is Grace, so her nickname is "Graceland".

My youngest child used to think her middle name truly is Graceland. This was not a problem until she was being tested to enter kindergarten. With all the "Katelyns" and "Brooklyns" out there, I would think "Graceland" sounded like a reasonable name. I know I have heard worse names. These teachers performing the test disagreed. When my daughter was asked to give her full name, she said "Graceland". I was then asked to give an explanation. I explained to them, and my daughter, that her name was actually Grace, not Graceland. Amazingly, I was the only one who found the story to be funny. My daughter found no humor at all in the misunderstanding. In fact she was quite upset about it.

I have found that telling funny stories about her also upsets her. She crosses her arms, stomps to her room, and yells, "It's not FUNNY!" For this and other reasons I have decided not to use my daughters' real names in this book. I am trying to protect myself from ending up on some talk show defending my parenting skills or lack of skills. From this point on, my daughters will be referred to as Elvis and Graceland.

Finding Jesus

When my daughter Elvis was in preschool, she never wanted to be herself. She was always pretending to be someone else, and that someone was always male. She pretended to be the real Elvis, Chinese Elvis, and Gaston from the <u>Beauty and the Beast</u> cartoon. She corrected anyone who called her by her real name. We got some odd looks from people, but most people humored her.

Then Elvis decided she wanted to be Jesus. I knew she meant well. After all, who could be a better role model? When we would go to the store or ran errands, people would stop to talk to us. (We live in a small town in Tennessee where this is a common occurrence.) The always friendly Elvis would converse for a moment and then announce, "I'm Jesus!" The strange looks we received before with Elvis's other pretend personalities were nothing compared to the reactions to her proclamations of being Jesus. Several people thought she was blaspheming. Others thought I was being blasphemous for allowing it.

In the past Elvis quickly moved on to a new identity if I did not make a big deal about who she was pretending to be. Each identity usually lasted a few days. This was not the case with her Jesus identity. Luckily her preschool teachers, Miss Sue and Miss Sheema, were very understanding. If they called Elvis by her real name, she reminded them that she was Jesus. Her teachers played right along.

The church where Elvis's preschool was held had a gym where I walked laps while she was in class. One day while I was walking laps, Elvis's class came into the gym to play. After playing for a while, the teachers decided it was time to line up. Elvis was the line leader that day, so Miss Sue asked all the children to line up behind "Elvis". Elvis said, "I'm Jesus." Miss Sue said, "Oh yes. Everyone line up behind Jesus!" Chaos followed. Fifteen little preschoolers ran around the gym. They looked and looked for Jesus. Since they could not find Jesus, they could not get behind Him. Miss Sue just stood there shaking her head. Finally she and Miss Sheema herded the children into a line.

Lesson Learned: If you are looking for Jesus, do not trust a bunch of preschoolers to show you the way.

Princess Leia Sightings

Once we told Elvis that she was going to be a big sister, she started picking out baby names. She had loved <u>Star Wars</u> ever since she could say the word "alien" and had an impressive collection of <u>Star Wars</u> action figures by age four.

With such inspiration, Elvis came up with two baby names. If a girl, her sister would be named Princess Leia. If a boy, her brother would be named Luke Skywalker. In Elvis' mind, no other names should even be considered. Doyle and I had to secretly discuss baby name options while Elvis was out of ear shot.

As my due date grew nearer, we tried to gently break it to Elvis that we were not going to use either of her baby name choices. This she refused to accept. She did not throw a fit. She simply stayed in a constant state of denial about the subject.

Doyle and I believe that children are to obey their parents and not the other way around. With that said, we called Elvis' new sister Princess Leia until she was about three months old. When people asked what the baby's name was, Elvis would proudly announce the name of that famous galactic princess. She was always disappointed by the negative responses it most often brought. Eventually, Elvis gave up the fight, and told me that we did not have to call her sister Princess Leia anymore.

Lesson Learned: Don't let Elvis name your baby.

The Name Game

When Graceland was about two and a half years old, she decided she did not like her name. That is when she changed her name to Cinderella Barbie Rapunzel Swimsuit Girl Oddette Katie Kat. (I am not kidding.) If someone did not call her all these names, she would usually let it slide, unless the offenders were her father or me. The two of us had to remember all the names and have them in the correct order.

I finally wrote all the names on our chalkboard in the kitchen, so I could just read off all the names when I needed to call Graceland or address her in some way. If I was not in the kitchen and did not have the list in front of me, I just called out "Hey you!"

One day Graceland said with a sigh, "It's OK. You don't have to call me Cinderella Barbie Rapunzel Swimsuit Girl Oddette Katie Kat anymore." Graceland finally realized that her parents' inability to remember names meant we were never going to remember all those names in the correct order. You could tell she was disappointed, but I was so relieved.

Lesson Learned: If you are going to change your name, don't make it too complicated.

Tougher Cinderella

Graceland eventually realized that not only her parents, but everyone else was unable to remember all the names that she wanted to be called. She was going to have to come up with a new way for people to address her. I had already dubbed her "Princess of Destruction", which she was very proud of until she found out what "destruction" meant.

Graceland was crazy about Cinderella, and we stalked Cinderella all over Disney World on our visit there. Graceland watched her Cinderella movie over and over again. Finally she came to the conclusion that she would stick with being called Cinderella, but there needed to be a change to the name. After all, Cinderella let everybody kick her around. As Graceland put it, Cinderella needed to be "more tougher". Therefore, Graceland wanted to forever more be known as "Tougher Cinderella."

Lesson Learned: Why didn't I notice such flaws in fairy tales when I was a child? Toughen up, Cinderella!

Chapter 7
Embarrassing Parenting Problems

Embarrassing Times at City Hall

Every year my church presents a living nativity at Christmas time. It is a really big deal for our small town. One of my jobs every year was to go to City Hall and get a permit to block off the street in front of our church, so pedestrians would not get mowed over by oncoming traffic.

This particular year was no different. I carried young Elvis on my hip as I walked into City Hall. She was probably only about a year and a half old. Elvis always noticed everything and felt she had to tell me about everything she saw. (She started talking very early.) I went straight to the long front counter in City Hall. Behind the counter were many desks and many people busily scurrying around. A clerk asked if she could help me, and I said, "I'm here for the First Baptist Church…" As I was trying to tell the clerk my mission, Elvis pointed behind me and said, "Fug. Fug." I had no idea what she was talking about, but I tried to continue talking to the clerk. This of course caused Elvis to get louder. She now was saying, "Fug you Mommy. Mommy, fug you!" Now all the people who had been scurrying around stopped what they were doing and started looking from Elvis to me and then to each other. One person even walked up to the counter and asked the clerk what I needed. I assume she wanted to hurry us out of the building. I then said, "As I was saying, I am

with the First Baptist Church and need a permit…"
"Fug you Mommy!" my child continued.

Finally the clerk handed me a form to fill out. (There is no form for blocking off a road in my town, so the clerk had to hand me some other form and scratched out the form's title. This had only added to the chaos of the situation.) Once I had the form and was heading out the door, I was able to give my child my full attention. She had been moving her legs from her knees down as if she were riding a horse, while I had been talking to the clerk. She had been trying to get me to walk over to a distant corner of the room. I finally realized that Elvis was trying to say "Flag! Mommy you look at the flag." in her little baby way.

Of course, it had sounded like church going Mom had been teaching her young child bad words and phrases. By the time I had discovered what Elvis was trying to tell me, no one in the office was paying any attention to us, so I loudly said, "You were trying to say "Flag". Yes, sweetie, that is a FLAG!." No employees paid any attention to me.

Lesson Learned: After taking Elvis to City Hall, plan on going next door to the Downtown Cafe and drowning your worries in a big piece of chocolate cheese cake and an enormous cheeseburger. (Yes, I strongly encourage this type of emotional eating when you have young children.)

Food is for Sharing

Elvis has always been a kind child and a little diplomat. She has always been good at smooth-talking her way out of things and has also always been a terribly picky eater. The combination of these traits has made for interesting meals at our house during her younger years.

Usually Elvis would shine when we had company. She would look down at her dinner plate with disgust. Elvis would then start to woo our guests. She would look sweetly at them and smile. When her father and I were not paying attention, Elvis would transfer her unwanted food over to our guest's plate. She would do this in such a way that our guest thought Elvis was selflessly sharing her food out of the kindness of her generous little heart. The food recipient would usually respond with an, "Oh, you are so sweet." or "What a kind child." The guest would typically make such a big deal over Elvis' generosity that her father and I hated to inform them that they had just been "had".

Elvis started using this redistribution of food technique when she was about 2 years old. By the time she was 5, she had mastered her technique.

Her picky eating habits continued as she grew. Some days, sweets were not even a good enough temptation for her. One day she came to me and said she was "so hungry". I told her I would give her an ice cream sandwich if she picked up her room. This was a bribe that usually worked. Elvis looked up at me and said, "I'm not hungry." Elvis came back later and said she was thirsty. I said, "pick up your toys, and I'll give you something to drink." She said, "Never mind. I'm not that thirsty."

Lesson Learned: Such willpower. Such determination. I hated that I had to pull out the Mom card and tell her to clean her room anyway.

Some Food Should Not Be Shared

Like many young children, Elvis would force large bites of food into her small mouth. On one such occasion, I told Elvis to take smaller bites. She repeatedly ignored me. Once again I said, "That is too big of a bite." Elvis responded with, "That's OK. I have a big mouth." Elvis did have chubby cheeks, and they looked like they could store a lot of food. She also was so convincing with her arguments. In this instance, however, I did not falter in my stand. "You do not have a big mouth." I insisted. With her mouth full, Elvis replied, "Yes I do. See?" Yes, I did see, and so did all the other people at the table.

Lesson Learned: Do not say anything during a meal that might cause Elvis to open her mouth.

Play Place Diplomacy

I was in McDonald's Play Place with Elvis when she was about three years old. She started playing with two little brothers whom she had never before met. The three of them were having a great time when the boys' mom announced that it was time for the boys to leave. Elvis went over to the mom and begged her to let the boys stay. The mom said, "No. They have to leave." Elvis tried to make a deal with the mom. (She has always been a deal maker.) Elvis asked, "Could you just leave one of them?" This seemed to catch the mom off guard. She stood there silently for a few seconds as if she were deciding which one to leave. Then she seemed to realize that such an arrangement would qualify her as a "bad mom". She finally shook her head and gave Elvis an absolute "No". Elvis could not understand this. In her mind, she had come up with the perfect compromise.

Lesson Learned: Maybe Elvis should consider mediation as a career.

Gators and Possums

Neither of my children required much sleep as babies. Elvis loved to be read to and rocked, so I read and rocked, and rocked and read to that child. It usually took about an hour of reading and rocking to get her to sleep. Then she would only sleep for about thirty minutes.

Sometimes when she was really hard to get to sleep, I would get sneaky. I would pull out the books that were way over her reading level. She would cry, "Not Anne of Green Gables!" I would innocently reply, "Oh yes, let's see what Anne is up to this time." I would start reading, and it would bore her to sleep every time.

Graceland, on the other hand, fought sleep fiercely. I could not read to her while I rocked her. I needed both hands free to hold her down. Rocking Graceland was like wrestling an alligator. If I were lucky enough to get her to sleep, I was so worn out that I needed a nap. For this reason, she earned the nickname "Gator".

I eventually gave up on rocking Graceland. Instead I put her in the car and tried to lull her to sleep with a car ride. I would drive and drive. Eventually Graceland's eyes would close and her head would droop to one side. I would head for home, park the car, and start unbuckling her car seat. About that time, Graceland would quickly open her eyes and look up at me. It always startled me like a scene in a horror movie. She was just playing possum again! This scenario happened often. For this reason she also earned the nickname "Possum".

After all attempts to get her to sleep failed, I would put her in her crib and leave her to cry herself to sleep. This rarely worked either, because she would cry so hard that she would throw up. Her cry always sounded a little different before she threw up. Doyle and I learned to recognize that cry very well. We would ignore her cries until the frequency changed. Then we would run to the nursery as if our lives depended on it. As soon as Graceland saw one or both of us, she would stop crying, but the sniffling and gasping would continue for about 30 more minutes.

Lesson Learned: I am going to be 80 years old before I catch up on lost sleep.

The Smell of Vinegar

When Graceland was a baby, she would hold onto the rails of her crib and jump up and down until I would come get her. I would get her out of the crib and would notice how her breath always smelled like vinegar. She was not old enough to eat solid foods, and she certainly had never had pickles. I could not understand why she had that smell.

One day when Graceland was about a year and a half old, we went to our local Lowe's store, and Doyle and I were asking a clerk for some assistance. Graceland was not behaving very well and was being rather ornery. The older clerk looked at Graceland then turned to Doyle and me and said, "I bet that kid spits vinegar!" My eyes grew wide. I asked, "How did you know?"

Lesson Learned: If your baby's breath smells like vinegar, consider it a warning of things to come.

Oh, For the Love of Shoes

Graceland has always loved shoes. This was painfully obvious at a very early age. She definitely inherited this from her Nana and Aunt Louise.

On one occasion, my daughters and I were at a doctor's office. We had already been waiting for about 20 minutes, and Graceland, who was about a year and a half old, was getting bored. She began walking around the somewhat crowded waiting room. She stopped in front of a lady. This woman was seated with her legs crossed. The one elevated foot was sticking out into the walkway a little bit. With her chin tilted down, Graceland shyly looked up at the lady with her big blue eyes. She was looking very angelic, and I started to worry. What was she up to?

The lady politely smiled. Graceland then looked down at the lady's elevated shoe for a few seconds and looked back up at the lady's face. The lady once again smiled at Graceland. Graceland again looked at the lady's foot. I knew Graceland was about to get into trouble. Finally she made her move. She grabbed the lady's shoe and made a run for it. I don't think she had thought out her escape route. There was nowhere for her to run except in a circle around the waiting room.

The poor woman just sat there with her mouth open. She did not know what to do. If she yelled at Graceland, she would sound like a baby hater, but she could not go around with just one shoe. Wide-eyed, she silently watched while I chased Graceland around an island of chairs in the middle of the room as if we were the last players in a game of musical chairs. Everyone else in the room just sat still and seemed confused. Once I caught her, I forced the reluctant Graceland to give back the shoe. The lady was noticeably relieved.

Lesson Learned: I will have to try harder to steer my children from future shoe crimes.

Fashion Statements

Before becoming a parent, I remember seeing children and wondering why on earth their parents would let their children leave the house dressed the way they were dressed. Now, I realize that as parents, we have to "pick our battles". Sometimes letting a child wear a crazy outfit to the store is better than the crying. There are times, however, when we have to put our foot down and be parents. There was a time that I wish my husband had done just that.

I was working late and there was a PTO meeting at our daughter's elementary school. My husband decided to attend the meeting with both our daughters.

I had just gotten home when the three of them returned from the meeting. As they walked into the house, I could see, to my horror, that my younger daughter had worn her favorite outfit, which included her "Groovy Girl" hip hugger jeans with bright colored ruffled fabric going around the legs. She was also wearing her blue floral bikini top that was too small and a camouflage do-rag. As you may have suspected, none of the patterns or colors matched on this outfit. The main problem, though, was that she looked like a 5-year-old biker chick. I asked, "Did you wear THAT to the PTO meeting?" My husband, in a very sarcastic way, said, "What do you think?" He was not aware of the great danger he was already in before he made that comment.

Yes, my daughter wore her do-rag, bikini top, hip hugger outfit in front of all the other moms at the elementary school. I could only pray that all the moms noticed that her father brought her, and that I was not present to veto the fashion statement.

I never heard any comments from the other mothers, but I know that Graceland's fashion statement did not go unnoticed. The next day at school, several children asked Elvis why her little sister wore just a bra to the PTO meeting.

Lesson Learned: If your husband takes your children out in socially unacceptable clothing, start a rumor about him being insane.

Chapter 8
Present Problems

Christmas Presents and Kitty Cat Costumes

One Christmas before Graceland was born, I "picked" Elvis' young brain for Christmas present ideas. "What should we get Daddy for Christmas?" I asked. "A reindeer costume!" was Elvis' answer. "Oh?! I don't know about that... Let's think of something else." I replied. "Let's get Daddy a kitty cat costume!" Elvis eagerly suggested. You could tell that she liked this idea even better. The harder I tried to talk Elvis out of the kitty cat costume, the more determined she was that her daddy needed a kitty cat costume for Christmas. Finally, I said, "Let's get Daddy a reindeer costume!" I figured this was at least a Christmasy present. Elvis was not convinced. I took her to the Christmas shop at a local store and found some headbands with reindeer antlers. I acted very surprised that we could not find any headbands with kitty cat ears in the Christmas shop. Elvis was noticeably disappointed at our inability to find that "perfect" gift for her dad. Finally Elvis reluctantly agreed to the reindeer antlers. She did not insist on any additional reindeer wear, because this present was obviously second rate.

When Doyle opened his present, he did not act very impressed. I took him aside and said, "You should be grateful and wear those antlers. It could have been a kitty cat costume."

Lesson Learned: Do not ask Elvis for present ideas.

Present Disappointment

After asking for Christmas present ideas for Daddy, I asked Elvis what she would like for Christmas. She said, "A naked guy, a magic carpet that works, and a blue wooden soldier that's not a nutcracker." The naked guy was no problem. This meant that Elvis wanted a Moses doll from the *Prince of Egypt* movie. He was only wearing a skirt and sandals. Aunt Louise wanted to buy Elvis the "naked guy", so we told her that was fine.

The magic carpet request was another way of saying "childhood disappointment". Doyle and I were set up for disaster with this present. I went to the fabric store and bought some fabric, ornate ribbons, and tassels. I thought the resulting doll size magic carpet looked impressive, but it did not fly, literally or figuratively.

As for the blue wooden soldier that was not a nutcracker, he could not be found. I looked high and low, but could only find nutcrackers. I could not even find a blue nutcracker. Finally I bought a nutcracker, painted his pants blue, and glued his mouth shut.

Christmas Eve arrived, and we made our annual trip to Aunt Louise's house for dinner. Aunt Louise gave Elvis her present. It was a rather long box that Elvis was unwrapping, which worried me. The naked guy box was much smaller. When Elvis opened it, she found a double box set that held Phoebus and Esmeralda from the *Hunchback of Notre Dame* movie. Aunt Louise leaned over and whispered to me, "Is that the right doll?" I said, "Well, uh…", but I was thinking, "That's not even the right movie, and these dolls are wearing clothes!"

The stores were already closed for Christmas, and Elvis was not going to get a single thing that she had asked for. To make things worse, our electricity was out because of an ice storm, and we were staying with my parents. They also had no electricity, but they had a wood burning stove. Both houses had electric water heaters, so there was no warm water to bathe. Even worse, Elvis had had a fever for three days. On Christmas Eve day, Elvis's pediatrician had said he was not sure if she had an ear infection or not. If she got worse, I was to call him, and he would call in an antibiotic. I tried to encourage him to go ahead and give me a prescription since it was Christmas Eve, and he would be out of the office and the drug store closed. He thought this suggestion was preposterous.

Elvis got worse. She did have an ear infection and was very sick on Christmas day. I also became sick. Elvis' pediatrician had the day off, and his partner refused to call in a prescription without seeing her, so the day after Christmas was spent in the pediatrician's office. We still did not have electricity or hot water, so we were sitting in the waiting room with dirty hair and wrinkled clothes.

Elvis' Christmas really was turning into some story line from a Dicken's novel, but she took it all in stride. She had gotten many gifts, and she liked them all. However, I overheard her talking to her Papa. She said, "Papa, I like my presents, but I didn't get a naked guy, my magic carpet won't fly, and I know my wooden soldier is really a nutcracker."

After Christmas, we went to the store and bought a "naked guy" and, to my surprise, he was on clearance.

Lesson Learned: Encourage your child to wish for easy to find gifts.

Pink Princess Scooters

I have learned over the years that life is a lot sweeter if I do not take my husband shopping with me. He hates shopping and if I take him along, no one has a good time.

When I want to go shopping, my girls and I load into the car and make a day of it, if we can - although school and work really get in the way of our shopping trips. My husband stays at home. He's happy, we girls are happy, and he usually does not even ask us how much money we spent. Life is grand!

One Christmas, however, my husband decided that he might actually need to be involved in a few of our key Christmas purchases. Our children were with my parents for the evening so we could buy their gifts and not get caught. I had saved buying the bigger Christmas presents until last, because they were harder to hide. These presents were also heavy. That is the main reason I agreed to my husband going with me. In my attempt to save my back, I forgot about my "No husband" shopping rule.

We went to our local super store that evening. The first thing on the shopping list was a pink princess scooter for our youngest daughter. The store had been displaying them right inside the entrance just two days earlier. We walked inside and stopped right where the scooters had been. There were no pink princess scooters. Trying not to panic, I asked the greeter if the scooters had been moved. She did not know.

Our search was on. We went to where the bikes and other scooters were kept. Sure enough, there were the pink princess scooters, but there were only three left. Quickly my husband scooped up one. Fear left my mind and was replaced by relief.

By now my husband was already bored with shopping. He told me he was going to the automotive department, and he started to walk away. I suggested we set a time and place to meet back up, but my husband rebels against such things.

I quickly found the rest of our Christmas presents and made my way to the automotive department. I carefully looked down each aisle but found no husband of mine. I looked down each isle again and again. Yes, this happens every time we go shopping together. I have few problems getting my children to stay close to me in a store, but my husband is like a wild child when turned loose in florescent lit buildings.

Finally I decided that I had had it. This was supposed to be a quick shopping trip, and I had presents to wrap while our children were out of the house. I walked up to the service desk and asked the sales associate if she would page my husband. She asked, "What would you like for me to say?" "Really? I can think of a lot of things for you to say." I replied. The sales associate gave me a pen and paper and told me to write it down. Over the PA system came the announcement, "Would Doyle Veazey, the man with the pink princess scooter, please report to the service desk? Your wife is waiting on you." I think the sales associate enjoyed that announcement almost as much as I did. There was no pretending that that message was not for him. Doyle could not deny hearing it, because there were so many people in that store that knew him. Someone was bound to direct him to the service desk for me. Oh, I knew I was in trouble.

Doyle thought having a meeting place made him look henpecked. I figured that, having it announced over the intercom in a small town store that Doyle Veazey carries around pink princess scooters for his wife who is now tracking him down, had to be worse. I was right. Doyle thought what I did was much worse. In fact he told me about it the whole way home. "It is Christmas time, and we knew most of the people in that store. How could you embarrass me like that? I can't believe..." He went on and on. I really tried to look remorseful, but I had to keep looking out the passenger window to keep him from seeing the smile on my face.

Lesson Learned: PA systems are great, and that sales associate is Awesome!

Chapter 9
Issues with Deciphering

Unmarried

Both my daughters are crazy about my parents. Luckily my parents live close to us and get to visit often. When Elvis was really young, she would get into deep thought while we were riding in the car. One day while in the car, out of the blue she said to me, "Papa is so nice and handsome." I said, "You should tell Papa. I bet he would like to hear that." Elvis shook her little head no and said, "I can't." "Why can't you?" I asked. Elvis thoughtfully replied, "If I tell him that, he'll unmarry Nana and want to marry me." I told her that, contrary to what some may believe, that sort of thing is not allowed in Tennessee.

Lesson Learned: Talk about having plenty of self-esteem. Elvis has it.

Deep Thinking

Elvis was reminiscing again in the car and said, "We've known Nana almost all our lives." I told her, "Since Nana is my mom and your grandma, I think we've known her even longer than that." Elvis nodded in agreement.

Lesson Learned: We have known Nana a long time!

Unexpected Questions

Another day we were driving down the street, and Elvis was pondering the universe. She asked, "Mommy, why don't you have hair up your nose like Daddy?" I pondered her question but did not know what to say. Instead I thought, "Probably the same reason I don't have hair shooting out my ears."

Lesson Learned: I need to count my blessings.

Chapter 10
So Many Funerals

Unrest in Mississippi

My husband's Grandma Veazey was one of my favorite people of all time. When she passed away, it was hard on everybody. At the funeral in the middle of Mississippi, my husband was to be one of the pall bearers, so he was sitting at the front of the little country church. This was the same church where his grandma had played the piano for many years.

The little church was very crowded because so many people who loved Grandma Veazey had come to pay their last respects. I was sitting about halfway back. Elvis was sitting next to me, and Graceland was in my lap. There wasn't enough room to sit the not-quite-one-year-old Graceland next to me. The pew was just too crowded.

The service started. All was going well until the dreaded happened. Graceland, the baby, was bored. You probably are wondering why I brought her to the funeral to begin with. There was no nursery provided at the church, and everyone we knew was at the funeral.

At first Graceland did not fidget too much. Suddenly Elvis let out with an, "Oh, she poked me in the eye!" Graceland gave me her, "…and I meant to, too" look. I quietly scolded her. A few seconds later, Elvis let out with another "Ow! She did it again!" Graceland giggled this time. There was not enough room on the pew to sit Graceland on the opposite side of me. Graceland had to stay in my lap. I tried holding her hands down; Graceland protested. I whispered, "Stop poking Sissy!" Graceland said nothing. A few seconds later, "Ow!" exclaimed Elvis. Elvis was now holding both eyes from pain and for protection.

I was now trying to hold onto both of Graceland's hands, and she was just as determined that I was not going to. Things went south from that point on. I finally just stood up in the middle of the funeral with my small bundle of a rascal in my arms and headed for the door. Elvis looked horrified. I told her to stay there. After I went outside, I realized that I had left a five-year-old to sit by herself surrounded by people she did not know in the middle of a funeral. She probably was not happy about that situation, but she was more likely to behave than the child I had taken with me.

After going outside and having a "talk" with Graceland, it became obvious that there would be no going back inside. Graceland had been storing up her rascalness, apparently, and decided that it all had to be unleashed at that moment in time. Yes, I spanked her. This meant we really had to stay outside then.

Lesson Learned: At the next funeral we go to, Elvis is wearing safety goggles.

More Funerals

After struggling with mini strokes for years, my Granny Siler passed away. We made the long drive to Pennsylvania for her funeral. Once again we had no one to watch Elvis or Graceland, who was now almost two years old. My husband stayed in Tennessee to work. My mom vowed to sit with my girls and me while Pop sat with the other pall bearers.

The funeral was at the Kegal Funeral home. This funeral home has little bowls of assorted candies scattered throughout the building. Mom and I snuck around collecting as many pieces as we could before the funeral.

When it was time for the funeral, we took our seats. We sat near the back of the room but were unable to get next to the aisle. The preacher got up and spoke a few words. Several of Pop's brothers had decided to get up individually and sing a song and say a prayer. Pop came from a big family.

Not long into the service, Graceland started getting anxious. Elvis was quietly sitting still and listening. I tried to quietly unwrap a piece of candy. I put it in Graceland's mouth. Being like their mother, my children love candy, but Graceland spit out the candy onto the floor a row in front of us and made a "Yuck" face. Mom frantically struggled to reach the rejected candy and wrap it up before it was permanently stuck to the carpet. Graceland continued to fidget and began talking to Mom and me. I unwrapped a piece of candy that was a different flavor from the first to bribe my child into behaving. Once again, she spit it to the floor and made a "Yuck" face. Mom chased down that piece of candy and wrapped it back up.

By this time one of my uncles had sung a song and was leading a prayer. After his prayer, he said "Amen". To this Graceland had to let out with a loud echo "Amen" just like she would at the dinner table. I could hear a few people in the back letting out quiet giggles. Then another uncle stood up and sang a song. Graceland had rejected every piece of candy that we had given her. A couple of pieces had landed two rows in front of us which led me to believe that someone had been practicing spitting watermelon seeds with her in the back yard. After the second uncle finished singing, he began to pray. My heart was filled with dread. Graceland was fidgeting terribly but did not seem to be paying attention. When my uncle finished, he also said "Amen". Graceland did not even look up, but yelled, "Amen!" More giggles could be heard this time.

A third uncle got up to sing. I began to count in my head, "How many more uncles were going to get up there?" Elvis was seated still as could be, but I looked like I was wrestling with a small alligator. This uncle sang a song and said a prayer. I cringed as he said, "Amen". Right on cue, Graceland yelled, "Amen!!" This time, people in the back of the room were laughing out loud. Graceland began to notice the response she was getting, and she liked it. A fourth uncle went up to the podium. Yes, you can guess what happened. The preacher then stood up and said, "Let us pray." I thought "Please don't."

This time Graceland proudly proclaimed, "Aaameen". She then began to play to her audience. Amazingly the preacher decided to speak more. I knew we could stay no longer. With Graceland in my arms, I climbed over several people's laps. Several of my relatives were trying to get me to leave Graceland behind for entertainment. One relative even grabbed her legs as I tugged in the other direction. I declined their offers and spent the rest of the funeral in the hallway with my little rascal.

Afterward several people told me that was the most fun they had ever had at a funeral. There were probably even more people who would have liked to have told me something else.

Lesson Learned: Am I paying for my raising?

Chapter 11
Complications with "I Love You"

Saying "I Love You"

Elvis has always been a smooth-talking diplomat. Before she was even in preschool, she had learned how to get out of trouble. When scolded, she would take me by the hand, look me in the eyes and say, "I love you, Mommy." She would then give me a big long hug. All that really messes up the effectiveness of my fussing.

Graceland, by about age three, had developed a different "I love you" technique than her sister's. If I fussed at her about something, she would walk away grumbling in an aggravated tone. I would ask, "What did you say?!" Graceland would turn around; look me in the eye and say, "I said I love you." "Oh really," was my reply, "it didn't sound like that." I may not have understood a word of her grumbling, but I knew that she was lying. What could I say? I could not say, "No you don't. What did you really say?" How could I punish her for what she really said, when I did not know what she really said? To make matters worse, she would give me a sweet smile, and often times would give me a kiss on the cheek after professing that she "loved me".

This situation always left me with mixed emotions. On the one hand, I do not like to be lied to. On the other hand, Graceland was so young to come up with such a clever comeback that I hated to squash her creativity. I never did figure out how to handle the situation. Eventually, Graceland just did her grumbling in her head.

Lesson Learned: There is no effective defense to "I love you".

Buried Treasure

One day Graceland and I were out in the yard. I was weeding flower beds when she called out to me, "I love you, Mommy." This threw up a big red flag in my brain like it would in the mind of any mom, so I walked over to Graceland. "What are you doing?" I asked. With a guilty look in her eye, she said, "I buried my shoes." "Would these be your brand new shoes that you just had to have?" I asked the tiny shoe queen. "Yes," she replied. She reassured me by saying, "But I know just where I buried them."

Lesson Learned: Children have similar instincts to dogs. They both bury their treasures.

Chapter 12
Wrong Conclusions

Elvis' First Love

When Elvis was about a year and a half old, we got a new Walmart in our town. It had a McDonald's restaurant in it and everything. As you walked in the entrance to Walmart, there was a park bench on the left with a life-sized Ronald McDonald seated on it. Ronald was made of some type of very strong plastic. Because of this big Ronald McDonald, I had to plan on my Walmart visits lasting at least an additional twenty or thirty minutes. Why? Because Elvis LOVED that Ronald McDonald. She would run to him with open arms and climb into his lap. She would kiss his cheeks and hands. This made me shudder. Who knew what all had been touching him? Elvis was unaware that there were other people around. Since we were at Walmart, there were plenty of other people around. I just stood there greeting customers like an unwanted chaperone. Elvis would just talk and talk to Ronald while she held his face gently in her hands. She never seemed to notice that he did not talk back. He was the strong, silent type.

These visits went on for months, until McDonalds pulled out of our Walmart. When McDonalds left, they took their seated Ronald McDonald with them. These were tragic times at our house. The love of Elvis' young life had left without saying goodbye.

Lesson Learned: You cannot depend on a clown.

Bar Problems

We were driving down the street one day when a song about a honky tonk came on the radio. (We live in Tennessee, so listening to country music on the radio is expected.) Elvis asked me what a "honky tonk" was. I did not want to elaborate too much, since my children were still at young ages. I simply said that a honky tonk was a place with a bar and a dance floor. Graceland, trying to be helpful, explained, "Like ballet lessons." I replied, "Well…no… it's a different kind of bar."

Questions Learned:

1. Do some honky tonks offer ballet lessons?
2. If you take ballet lessons at a honky tonk, does that make you a redneck?

Unusual Conclusions

When Elvis was about four years old, she asked me, "If it's night here, is it morning in China?" What?!" Where did that come from? I asked if they had been talking about that at preschool. Elvis said "No". Had they been talking about that on PBS? Again Elvis said, "No."

I talked to Elvis' preschool teacher, who said her class had not been talking about time zones, China, or anything relating to Elvis' question.

How can a small child theorize about time zones when grown men of long ago civilizations could not understand that the world was round?

Lesson Learned: How long is it going to be before Elvis figures out that she is smarter than her parents?

Chapter 13
Restrooms Predicaments

Public Restroom Predicaments

Going to public restrooms while shopping could truly be a challenge with my family. Any mom knows how difficult using a public restroom can be when your children are young. The situation can only get more difficult if the mom also needs to use the restroom herself.

There I would be, in a crowded bathroom. The stalls would be too small to house me and the stroller my child was in. When I needed to use the restroom myself, I tried handling this situation in several different ways. I tried taking my child out of the stroller and having her stay in the stall with me. Yes, this had disaster written all over it. My oldest daughter has always been very sociable. Every time that I would try this bathroom technique, Elvis would get down on that probably filthy floor and crawl into the next stall. The whole time I would be trying to grab one of her limbs and would tell her, "No, No, No, come back!" My attempts always failed because Elvis was on a mission. Once in another stall, she would attempt to befriend the shocked lady in that stall. She would always ask, "What your name?" The lady would usually answer with something like, "Hi there?…little girl. Go back to your mommy."

Elvis would ignore this request and would continue to ask for the lady's name. No lady ever gave her name. I suppose they were afraid to give too much information, but really what else did they have left to hide? The most awkward part was getting Elvis out of the stall. I really did not want to crawl in the stall after her for more reasons than one, so I would reach my arm under the wall and look for a foot or something familiar. Elvis wanted to stay, so she would dodge my lunges. I would finally grab a limb and drag her back to me.

I finally tried a new bathroom technique. I decided to keep Elvis strapped in her stroller while in the bathroom. Of course this worked best if there is a handicapped stall. (I apologize to all the disabled people who get aggravated at people like me for tying up these stalls.) If there is no large stall, your options are limited. I am too paranoid to leave the stroller and baby outside of my stall. The stalls were always too small, and the doors opened into the stall. This left me with one option: leave the stall door open with the stroller sticking out into the walk way. Of course I would always try to use the last stall, but some curious person always had to see what was going on at the other end of the bathroom. I decided to just act like this was all very normal and greeted the curious onlooker with a friendly "Hello" as if I were a greeter at Wal-Mart.

Lesson Learned: When you go shopping with small children, take a friend to help with the baby, or give up shopping for a few years.

Oh, Those Public Restrooms

When my youngest daughter was newly potty trained, she had an unusual fondness for public bathrooms. As soon as we would get in a building that was new to her, she would say, "I have to go potty." I would ask her if she was sure. She was always sure. We would walk in the bathroom, and she would look around. Whether she decided she needed to "go" depended on her impression of the bathroom. If it did not look stylish enough, she would say, "I'll hold it." My response was always, "Oh no, you won't!"

Lesson Learned: Don't potty train your children until they are 20.

Toilets Should Not Be Automatic

My two children were horribly afraid of self-flushing toilets. All three of us would end up in one tiny stall taking turns. I would cover the censor with my hand while each child took turns pottying. My younger child would always complain that I was crowding her, as if I really wanted to be standing in such an uncomfortable position between the toilet and the wall while I leaned over to cover the sensor and tried to keep my balance.

I think God occasionally gives me good ideas to help me preserve my sanity, because one day the solution came to me. Each time we went into a restroom with self-flushing toilets, I gave each child a big sticker from my daughters' sticker stash that always mysteriously ended up in my purse. My girls would cover the sensor with their sticker, so the toilet would not flush on its own. When my girls were done, they just pulled the sticker off the sensor. From then on, we each could use our own stall, and no one fussed about having to take turns.

Lesson Learned: Stickers Rock!

Drainage

I was washing my hands at home one day and noticed white stuff sticking out of the sink drain. I started to remove the white stuff and figured out that it was very small pieces of cotton. My thoughts went straight to my youngest daughter. I called this same daughter into the bathroom and asked her to tell me why there was cotton in the drain. She immediately confessed. She had decided to pluck all our Q-tips bald, although she never clearly explained why. Graceland had already realized that I noticed what was put into the trash can, so she had decided to hide the evidence by stuffing the cotton down the drain. Unfortunately, I got the feeling that cotton was not all that she had stuffed down the drain. I think the vein in my forehead must have been sticking out, because she clammed up and would not give me any more information.

Lesson Learned: Those teenage years are going to be terrible.

Shower Problems

I believe it is safe to say that most people expect their time in the bathroom to be their private time. This was not often the case in my house. Most mothers of young children can relate to this. Like most moms, I would try to sneak into the bathroom for a quick shower before my children realized I was missing. My youngest daughter used to often catch me, however. I would be enjoying my too hot shower when my stealthy daughter in one quick jerk would pull back the shower curtain similar to the shower scene in *Psycho*. I would scream while she shoved some broken toy at me and said, "Fick it Mommy! Fick it!" The answer was always the same. "Not right now!" I cannot complain too much about Graceland's shower curtain habit though, because she inherited the tendency from me.

Lesson Learned: Fix all broken toys before getting in the shower, or just lock the door and let the kids stand out in the hallway crying.

Toothbrush Time

I began brushing my teeth one day when I noticed that my toothbrush tasted odd. Fear suddenly went through my mind, so I went to my daughter's bedroom. I politely and calmly asked, "Have you been using Mommy's toothbrush?" Very matter-of-factly she said, "Yes." "On your teeth?" I asked. She said, "No.' "What have you been cleaning with Mommy's toothbrush?" I asked. She replied, "Things in the bathroom." My mind began to race as I imagined what she may have scrubbed with MY toothbrush. I then asked her to show me what she had cleaned. By now the vein must have been popping out of my forehead, because she suddenly started acting concerned for her safety. I tried to act calmly and reassure her. I let her know that I needed to know what she had cleaned with MY toothbrush. I am guessing that my face must have been red by now too, because it was obvious that she was not going to tell. She would only confess to scrubbing her dolls with it. By the guilty look on her face, I am guessing there had been some toilet scrubbing that got worked into the cleaning session. Of course she got the "Toothbrushes are for teeth only, and you can only use your own toothbrush" lecture, and I threatened her with a paddling if she ever touched my toothbrush again.

Lesson Learned: Mouthwash is my good friend.

More Shower Troubles

One day I was cleaning house when I heard screams coming from the upstairs bathroom. I ran upstairs and found my 5-year-old daughter looking sheepish and guilty. When I asked what had happened, 10-year-old Elvis told me that Graceland "...threw a pitcher of cold water on me. She just yanked back the shower curtain and threw it on me!" With head down as if ashamed, Graceland sported a sly smile that could still be seen. I was trying so hard not to laugh, that I made myself fake a cough. That way I could cover up the smile on my face with my hand and disguise my laugh with the cough. I shook my finger at Graceland, but couldn't say a word. I walked out of the bathroom. My eyes were watering so badly, I could hardly see my way down the stairs. I was coughing all the while until I finally made it downstairs and laughed out loud.

I later asked Graceland where she got that idea. She sincerely said she had just thought it up herself. She had never even heard of pouring cold water over the curtain rod onto the victim below. As bad as it sounds for a parent to think this, I think Graceland's prank was pretty clever for a preschooler.

Lesson learned: The next time I want to scare my mom in the shower with a water gun, I'm sending in Graceland to do the job.

Chapter 14
Clever Conclusions and Comebacks

I have a strong weakness for sweets, but my husband has an even stronger weakness for coffee. When I ask him how many cups he has had on any given day, he will say, "One." That means his first cup was never completely empty before he filled it up again and again. He just has one continuous cup all day every day.

When we go out to eat, Doyle always asks for, "…a cup of coffee, straight." Of course that means a cup of black coffee.

It came as no surprise that our oldest daughter has always loved coffee as well. At a restaurant one time, the waitress asked to take our drink order. Doyle ordered his straight cup of coffee. I ordered my usual boring glass of water and lemon. Ordering for herself, the then little Elvis said, "I want coffee, bent." Doyle, the waitress, and I all raised our eyebrows over that one. The waitress looked questioningly at me. I looked at Elvis and asked something analytical like, "What?" Elvis then tried to explain in her little person way. She said, "I don't like mine straight. I like it bent." At this, the light bulb turned on in my head. "She wants cream and sugar," I explained, "and decaf!" From then on when we went out to eat, little Elvis would ask for bent coffee. I loved the looks she would always get.

Eventually Elvis grew out of asking for bent coffee. I hate it when that happens.

Lesson Learned: If you want to strike up a
conversation, ask your server for bent coffee.

More Clever Comebacks

I have two clever little girls who can come up with some clever comebacks. On one occasion we had some out-of-town guests come for a visit. One of our guests believed that children should be seen and not heard. There were about eight of us at the supper table, and Elvis was talking a lot to everyone, as usual. You could tell that our guest did not approve. Elvis was only about 5 or 6 years old and was missing 2 front teeth. Our guest had been having some dental problems of his own and was also missing a front tooth.

Finally our guest had had enough of Elvis' talking, and he asked her, "What's wrong with your mouth? What happened to your teeth?" He was very pleased with his comment and started laughing. My daughter ignored his question and innocently asked, "What happened to yours?" His smile quickly faded, and everyone else's eyebrows went up. The room went silent and all the other grownups lowered their heads to hide their smiles. I'm sure he expected me to scold her, but I was so impressed with her comeback, I couldn't. As the saying goes, "Out of the mouths of babes come pearls of wisdom."

Lesson Learned: Don't make fun of a child's toothless grin if you have one yourself.

Batman Problems

My older daughter always loved her superhero action figures and would often play with them in the car. While going down the road one day, she was in the back seat playing with her Bibleman and Batman action figures. Bibleman, who fights the bad guys with God's Word, was sternly talking to Batman. Finally Bibleman asked Batman, "Are you a Christian, Batman?" Batman replied in a very hateful non-Batman tone, "No, I'm not!" In a very deep voice, Bibleman replied, "Then you're going to HELL!"

Lesson Learned: That Bibleman is one tough superhero.

Clever Solutions

I had pretty well childproofed our house before our youngest daughter was born. There were still two kitchen drawers that were not completely safe, and one bathroom makeup drawer that was off limits. My youngest daughter as well as my oldest daughter knew this, but Graceland had stronger rascal tendencies when it came to the forbidden. Following these tendencies, Graceland would get into these forbidden drawers anyway.

It was during this time that I discovered that Graceland was afraid of plastic spiders and plastic spider rings that people give out at Halloween. Every Halloween we would end up with several of these plastic spiders. Graceland was tall enough to reach into the forbidden drawers, but she was not tall enough to see into them. I came up with plan. I placed several plastic spiders into the forbidden drawers, but did not tell Graceland. She would sneak into the bathroom or the kitchen. Opening the drawer, she would reach in. Because she was unable to see what she was grabbing, several times she pulled out a spider. Each time she would scream and come looking for me. She would take me to the scene of the crime and exclaim, "Pider! Pider!" I asked, "Why were you in that drawer?" It was obvious that she thought that I was missing the point and would go on to explain about the bigger picture that I needed to be focusing on, the spider. This same scenario happened several times. Finally Graceland stopped coming to get me. I would just hear her scream. The screams usually would be coming from the bathroom. I would then run to her and find her standing there with a scowl on her face. She would fuss at me and say, "Pider!" She really was getting rather aggravated that I was not fixing our "pider" problem. She also did not like how this spider problem was getting her into trouble.

Eventually the spiders mysteriously disappeared. I was surprised that it took as long as it did. The absence of spiders meant the makeup drawer was left unguarded. One day I found Graceland walking around with a bright red lipstick mustache. I asked her if she had been in the makeup drawer. Of course she said "No". I decided that it was time for a family portrait in the kitchen, so I gathered Graceland, Daddy, and Elvis around the kitchen table. Doyle took one look at Graceland with raised eyebrows and said nothing. I looked at him and said, "I think we need to take a family picture." Doyle immediately figured out my plan. I was collecting evidence to be used at a future date, as in a future date with a boy. Elvis did not even notice Graceland's mustache, so the picture turned out wonderfully.

Lesson Learned: If you use plastic spiders as a deterrent, be prepared to pay for therapy during your child's grown up years.

More Spider Problems

One day a few years later, both my daughters had decided to go for a walk on our property. They always carried their walking sticks just like their daddy. They each had their very own special walking stick that no one else was allowed to carry. I was working in the yard when my youngest child came running out of the garage with her sister's walking stick in hand. She was noticeably upset and told me, "There's a spider on my walking stick!" This was a real spider, and I had nothing to do with its being on her walking stick. I told her to "just kill it". After all, in the south we have plenty of spiders. I always choose to deal with them by killing them.

While Graceland and I were discussing her dilemma, Elvis came running out of the garage. She had seen Graceland with her walking stick. (In Graceland's defense, she would often get both walking sticks, so her big sister did not have to get hers. She often alternates between periods of schmoozing her sister and aggravating her.) Elvis exclaimed, "That is my stick! Yours is in the garage." Without hesitation and in a very defiant tone, Graceland said, "I'll give you your stick if you go get mine." I said nothing, but stood there in worried anticipation for what would happen next. Elvis let out a sigh of irritation, but ran into the garage and retrieved the walking stick. She never saw the spider. To Elvis' dismay, Graceland examined her stick carefully. After seeing no spider, she handed over Elvis' stick. Elvis said nothing.

With eyebrows raised, I said nothing. Graceland also said nothing. Graceland did not brag about her trick. She simply ran off to play with her sister.

Lesson Learned: Should I be worried or impressed?

Terrorist Problems

I know everyone remembers the terrible day of 9/11/2001. After the attacks, we still did not know if the whole nation was under attack. Were there more attacks to come?

Our younger daughter's preschool classes were canceled, and my husband's work closed, so the three of us sat at home in front of the TV. Should we pick up our older daughter, Elvis, early from grade school? Doyle decided that if there were more attacks to come that she might be safer in a school building.

I did not know what Elvis had heard, if anything, when I picked her up from school. When she got in the car, I asked her if she knew what had happened that day. Apparently the teachers at her school had heard something was happening in New York and had turned on the TV's in the classrooms. Once people started jumping from the Twin Towers windows, Elvis' teacher turned the TV off.

Elvis wanted to know why these men wanted to crash airplanes into buildings. I tried to explain what little I knew at the time in a way that a six year old would understand. I told her that these men do not believe in Jesus, and do not like us because we do.

As serious as she could be, Elvis said, "I know what we should do. We should catch these bad guys, tie them up, get the police to handcuff them and then..." I was expecting a description from some violent cartoon, but she totally surprised me. Elvis continued, "When we have them tied up, we should tell them about Jesus!" What a great idea! The terrorists would think it was some form of horrible torture, but we would be telling them what they really needed to hear. I think Elvis had a great idea.

Lesson Learned: Maybe we should let children solve the world's problems. They might do a better job than we are doing.

Bethlehem's Star

I used to sing in a church ensemble, and we always sang at least a couple of songs each Christmas at our church's Living Nativity. Back when Graceland was about four years old, our ensemble was practicing to sing a song called *Bethlehem's Star*. I listened to my practice tape in the car constantly. This was fine with Graceland, because she loved the song.

One day while driving down the road and listening to that song, Graceland said, "I bet Jesus dances when he hears us sing that song."

Lesson Learned: We really do need to have hearts like children.

Pretty Problems

I am sure it is common for complete strangers to walk up to a mother and her young daughter and tell the girl how pretty she is. My daughters are no exception to such occurrences. They have been told they are pretty countless times. Graceland eventually just accepted such comments as well-known facts and gave the well-intended flatterer a nod of polite acknowledgement.

One day I was fixing Graceland something to eat. As I handed her a plate, she looked up at me and sweetly said, "Mommy, I wish you were as pretty as me." I smiled and politely said, "Me, too."

Lesson Learned: Raising children can make you feel like the Cinderella who can't make it to the ball. You do all the work with no play and look ragged.

Seeing Problems

My dad has had terrible vision for years. When I was a kid, we would go swimming, and my dad would always swim, too. This was a problem because he had to take off his glasses. This meant he had to keep one hand in front of him at all times so he would not swim into anything. Pop never seemed to mind. His need for glasses was just a permanent part of his life.

Pop's birthday was coming up, and I was out of birthday present ideas. After much thought, I started seeking others' opinions on the subject. I asked Graceland what we should give Papa for his birthday. (I was secretly dreading the answer, because I was afraid of getting an answer similar to Elvis' suggestion for a kitty cat costume.) Graceland, in her grown up 4-year-old way, said, "Papa needs swimming glasses!" Swimming Glasses? I called our local Horner Rausch Optical and asked if they could get prescription swimming goggles. They said they could order them.

Before we knew it, Papa had the ugliest pair of goggles ever, but for the first time in his life, he could see while swimming.

Lesson Learned: I finally know who to ask for gift ideas. Seek the knowledge of the youngest.

Graceland and the Alien

We live close to the Space and Rocket Center in Huntsville, Alabama, so we occasionally go for a visit. The Space and Rocket Center has a rather large gift shop, as all places of learning should. I believe the gift shop is the real reason why my girls wanted to go there to begin with. (Well, Graceland also really enjoyed walking on the "moon" there.)

On one visit to the shop when Graceland was about three years old, Elvis brought her money and was prepared to buy a rather large stuffed "alien" that she had seen before. This led Graceland to believe that she also needed a similar stuffed alien. I asked her if she had enough money. Graceland explained that she was planning on me buying it. I then explained to Graceland that if she wanted it, she was going to have to buy it herself. Graceland had enough money, but she hated to part with it. She sobbed, "I'm going to miss you, alien." and put him back on the shelf.

Lesson Learned: It is so much more fun to shop with someone else's money.

Cat Calls

I always get annoyed when groups of men feel the need to make "cat calls" at women. I began to notice that after I reached a certain age that I received cat calls only when I drove my husband's old beat up truck. I thought this was very odd. It never failed, though. Every time I drove that rusty old thing, men whooped and hollered at me. I finally figured it out. These guys must have figured that any woman who would drive an old truck like that must have a boat to go with it.

Lesson Learned: If you are a woman desperate for a date, get an old truck with a "Gone Fishing" bumper sticker. You'll have men lined up at your door, but they might not be "keepers".

Checkout Problems

I was standing in the checkout line of my local Radio Shack one day. There was a nice looking man in line behind me, and I noticed that the sleeves of his shirt were ripped off. I did not think that much about it, and I just went back to waiting my turn in line. A few seconds later, in walked one of the scariest guys I had ever seen. He had all kinds of chains hanging off his black baggy clothes. He had multiple piercings on his face, and he was covered in tattoos. He immediately got in line behind the sleeveless man. Scary man then said to sleeveless man, "Hey, you look just like "Larry the Cable Guy." It was painfully obvious that sleeveless man was insulted, and he told scary guy as much. I was glad sleeveless man was brave enough to stand up for himself, but I figured bloodshed was soon to follow.

I am not sure what made me do it, but I turned around to face sleeveless man. I began jumping up and down and clapped my hands together. I then excitedly said, "Hey aren't you Brad Pitt?!" Sleeveless man started laughing. Scary guy looked confused. I grabbed my purchase and headed for the door. Sleeveless guy yelled to me, "Thanks a lot. I needed that!" Scary man continued standing in his confusion, and the tension in the air floated away.

Lesson Learned: Just because a guy looks like a redneck does not mean he likes to be called a redneck.

Brick Shortages

When we moved to the house in which we now live, it was like having a garden shop in our own yard. I did not necessarily like the way the flower beds and plants were arranged, but I liked most of the plants. We did not have to buy much of anything for the yard. We just rearranged things. I reduced the number of flowers beds and put similar flowers together. Doyle and I made a patio area out of paving stones that were scattered throughout the yard. We gave away unwanted plants and scalloped boarder bricks that were in the yard, except for the curved border bricks. I decided to put those in a circle around our mailbox, but found that I did not have enough of them.

I went down to our local garden shop and stood in the checkout line. As I waited, I looked in a book that gave the descriptions and barcode numbers of all the items in their stockyard. What do you know? I found the curved scalloped boarder brick I was looking for. There were a number of people in line behind me. I suppose they all had been inspired to work in their yards as well. It was finally my turn. I showed the clerk the item in the book and said, "I just need one of these." The clerk looked on the counter to see what else I had to buy and found nothing. Surprised, she looked at me and said, "You only want to buy one brick?" With a straight face, I said, "Well I only need one. They say I'm only one brick shy of a load." (No, really. I said that.) The clerk did not get it, but, judging from the chuckles behind me, I could tell the people in line did. When I turned toward them and pumped my eye brows at them, they realized it was OK to laugh, and they did.

Lesson Learned: You don't get to use classic lines like that every day.

Chapter 15
Awkward Moments

I always liked Elvis Presley's music when I was growing up. I even liked his movies, but I have never been what I consider an Elvis fanatic. I cannot say the same for my children. I suppose giving them the nicknames that I chose are really ironic choices.

One day when my Elvis was watching TV, the TV showed a clip of Elvis Presley singing at one of his concerts in his gold thread suit. My Elvis saw it and said, "Mommy, can you get me one of him for Christmas?" This was the beginning of her love for Elvis.

For her fifth birthday, Elvis had an Elvis Presley birthday party. I tried to get an Elvis impersonator. I thought the grownups would really get a kick out of that. Unfortunately, the impersonator had gotten too big for his Elvis suit. Talk about irony.

Graceland was quick to follow in her sister's Elvis obsession, so my husband and I decided to take a trip to Memphis. Our youngest daughter was very excited. Graceland was about two years old and had made all kinds of plans for our Memphis trip. "We're going to spend the night at Elvis' house, and he's going to fix me breakfast." She told me. I tried very hard to gently explain that those things could not happen, because Elvis had died. (Of course there were other flaws in her plans, but I did not see the point in trying to explain all that to a two year old.) As would be expected from a true Elvis Presley fanatic, Graceland refused to believe that Elvis was dead.

Once in Memphis, we did the usual tourist things. We went to see the true Graceland. We also went to the Peabody Hotel to watch the ducks waddle through the lobby on their way to the fountain. While waiting on the ducks, Graceland and I did one of my favorite things. We went to the hotel bakery.

(I suppose I should mention that everyone in my family has a low voice, and by that I do not mean that we speak softly. Graceland's voice may end up being the lowest voice of us all.).

The clerk in the bakery had her back to us, so she did not notice us walk in. Graceland and I walked up to the very tall counter.

As I looked toward the clerk, Graceland started talking. The clerk turned and looked at me. I looked at her. She heard a voice, but my lips were not moving. Her eyes opened very widely. She quickly hopped on the counter and leaned over it as far as she could. She seemed very relieved when she saw Graceland. I must have looked alarmed. After all it isn't every day that someone looks like they are going to do some kind of ninja move on my child and me.

"I didn't know who was talking." she explained. "She sure has a low voice. I thought she was a midget or something." By her reaction, I am guessing that she is afraid of little people.

After satisfying our sweet tooth, Graceland and I went back out to wait on the ducks in the hotel lobby. We were still discussing the real Elvis, and

Graceland was still refusing to believe that he was dead. I told her that a lot of people still have that problem, but that he was indeed dead.

As we were waiting on those ducks, who should walk up? An Elvis impersonator. When my two year old saw him, she said, "See Mommy. I told you Elvis isn't dead!" At this, I gave up. She had won. To Graceland, that man was Elvis.

Lesson Learned: Those trouble-making Elvis impersonators!

So Many Awkward Moments

I know from experience that if you have the problem of being shy, having children should take that problem away.

Elvis helped me to overcome my once painful shyness. Unfortunately, the cure was painful also.

Elvis was an extremely observant child. Her mind was truly like a little sponge, and she constantly soaked up everything she saw and heard. Elvis used to feel the need to share her newfound wisdom with me constantly. On one such occasion, we had driven to Murfreesboro, Tennessee, to meet several family members for dinner. The restaurant put several tables together to accommodate our large group. We were all seated and having a nice visit, when the almost two-year-old Elvis saw something that she thought was quite amazing. Elvis pointed to a lady at a nearby table and said in a loud voice, "Big Hair, Momma. Momma, Big Hair!" Sure enough, seated at the table next to us was a lady with the biggest hair that I have ever seen. No head of hair was ever teased more than that head of hair. I tried to calmly lower my child's arm with the pointing finger and whisper to her that, "Yes, I see the Big Hair." Apparently Elvis did not believe that I truly saw it, because I was not acting shocked enough.

She continued to point at the woman and exclaim, "Big Hair, Momma! Momma, Big Hair!" No matter how hard I tried to hush her, Elvis kept proclaiming about the "Big Hair". At one point she stood in her highchair and turned around toward the woman, so she could better show us where to find the "Big Hair".

I was trying not to look at the woman and hoped she did not know what the commotion was truly about. One quick glance at her face told me that she knew whose hair Elvis was referring to, and she looked annoyed.

It became obvious that I was going to have to take Elvis to the Ladies' room for a "talk". It did not appear that she had a clue that I truly wanted her to be quite. As I picked her up however, she quickly assured me, "Mommy, I be quiet! I be quiet!" That rascal finally was quiet.

Lesson Learned: A friend once gave me this bit of wisdom. The bigger the hair, the smaller the town. The woman at the restaurant must have come from a tiny town.

Dental Problems

Elvis has been overly blessed with cavities in her lifetime. Luckily, she loves her dentist. We regularly have her teeth cleaned, and she actually looks forward to it. On one such visit, we were called back to the examining room. The hygienist was ready for us. We were led to a large room with several reclined dental chairs. Each chair came with its own hygienist. Most of the hygienists at this dental office were serious by nature and rarely smiled. I often tried to get them to crack a smile, but usually only got a raised eyebrow. Elvis was asked to lie back in the chair. The hygienist got her tools ready and asked Elvis to open her mouth. To my surprise, instead of seeing Elvis' pretty smile, her teeth were covered with her plastic vampire teeth. I was shocked, and so was the hygienist. For a brief second, the hygienist actually cracked a smile. A miracle of sorts had just happened. It passed quickly, however, her smile faded and in a serious tone she said, "Take those out."

Lesson Learned: I never knew my daughter could make me so proud with plastic vampire teeth.

Piercing Problems

Two-year-old Graceland had been begging me and begging me to let her get her ears pierced. She was also begging and begging to chew gum. I was having a hard time potty training her, so I told her that only "big girls" get their ears pierced and chew gum. (My definition of a big girl was one who is potty trained.)

These two bribes helped greatly to speed up the inevitable and permanent dismissal of diapers from Graceland's life. After two weeks without diapers, Graceland reminded me of our deal.

There are only two places in our small town that pierce ears, so Graceland and I went to one to check things out. Unfortunately, Graceland started getting scared, so we went home unpierced. A few days later, Graceland started talking again about getting her ears pierced. She decided that she wanted to get her ears pierced the next day.

I did not realize that Elvis secretly called my parents and Aunt Louise and invited them to come watch the big event. The next day arrived, and we decided to have Graceland's ears pierced at our local Walmart. When we got there, Graceland found an audience waiting for her. One thing that the already reluctant Graceland hates is an audience. She was having serious thoughts of turning and running, but Aunt Louise and Nana Dot talked her into being brave. I filled out the necessary paperwork and paid for the piercing. All was going well until the sales associate put on her rubber gloves. Because of visits to the doctor's office, Graceland had learned to associate rubber gloves with pain, and she started crying.

To make things worse, a mentally-challenged lady appeared on the scene. Her speech was very difficult to understand, but it was apparent to me that she wanted to talk Graceland out of piercing her ears. She got awkwardly close to my shy child's face, and started shaking her head and saying, "No." This scared Graceland and she started crying louder. The situation went south from there. My mom and Aunt Louise misunderstood what the stranger was trying to say, and Nana went over to the woman and said, "Graceland, this lady is going to get her ears pierced today too."

This comment threw the woman into a panic. She thought we were going to force her to get her ears pierced as well. This distressed stranger started twirling around, flailing her arms, shaking her head, and yelling, "No". Graceland was sobbing by now. The two sales associates stood by wide-eyed, with piercing guns in hand. They did not know what to do and were afraid they were going to have to pierce a sobbing child and a screaming woman.

Several people turned toward the jewelry department to see what all the commotion was about. I was pretty sure most of the onlookers were talking about what a horrible mom I was, because I was forcing my poor child to pierce her ears. I knew these onlookers were unaware that chaos follows my mom and Aunt Louise wherever they go.

We were finally able to calm down the lady, but Graceland was still crying. She could not decide what to do. I told the clerks to "Just do it!" I did not want to go through all this again, and I was not leaving the decision to pierce or not to pierce up to Graceland. One clerk pierced one ear while the other clerk pierced the other. One clerk was so shaken by the whole incident that she missed the mark on Graceland's ear. (Graceland refused to have it redone, so her earring sets cock-eyed in that ear.)

After the piercing was done, Graceland was mad as could be, and she wanted to take her new earrings out right then just to spite me. However, Nana and Aunt Louise talked her out of performing any earring removals.

I had promised Graceland a new toy once her ears were pierced, because I knew it was going to hurt. Graceland led Nana, Papa, and Aunt Louise to the toy department. Elvis and I followed. Someone grabbed a buggy, and Graceland started piling in the toys. No one tried to stop her or limit her choices. We were all too traumatized from the previous thirty minutes. We all needed a new toy, some chocolate, or a sedative.

One of my eyes was twitching, and my head was pounding.

The stranger was now following us around. We were her new friends, but we could not understand a word she said. Finally she grew tired of repeating herself and walked away.

Lesson Learned: I hate potty training!

Paci Problems

Once potty training was out of the way, our next challenge was getting rid of Graceland's nighttime pacifier. Years earlier, I had talked Elvis into giving her pacifiers to Santa, so he could give them to babies who needed them. Elvis liked that idea. Graceland, however, did not. Graceland told me right away that those babies needed to get their OWN paci's. She also said she did not like Santa and did not want him coming into her house. If he had anything for her, she said he could leave it on the front porch.

Lesson Learned: Santa should probably skip our house for more than one reason.

Tooth Fairy Problems

We often had problems with the tooth fairy at our house. She sometimes would forget to come by for days on end. It has taken her as long as a week to leave money for a tooth. However, she always wrote a nice apology letter full of fairy tale excuses.

There was one thing the tooth fairy did that Elvis really liked. In addition to giving a couple dollars for each tooth, she also gave a collectible coin for each tooth. However, there was another thing about the tooth fairy that Elvis really did not like. She did not like to give up her teeth to the tooth fairy.

Elvis does not like to get rid of anything, trash included. She gets this from my mom and Aunt Louise. The whole idea of selling your teeth to the tooth fairy made Elvis uneasy. Once after losing a tooth, Elvis became very stressed about whether or not to put her tooth under her pillow. After all the tooth fairy would know to come because her fairy computer would tell her that Elvis had lost a tooth and would print out a map to Elvis' house. (according to Rachel's imagination)

Elvis came up with an ingenious plan. Instead of putting her tooth under the pillow, she put two $1 bills and a note. The note explained that she wanted to keep her tooth, but trade the $2 for a cool tooth fairy coin. Amazingly, the tooth fairy took the money and left a nice Italian coin.

A month or so later when I came home late in the evening from choir practice, (no really, I was at choir) my girls had already gone to bed. They were both sleeping in Elvis' bed. Doyle warned me as soon as I came in the door, "The girls are expecting a visit from the tooth fairy tonight."

"Did someone lose a tooth?" I asked. "No, Elvis had Graceland leave some $1 bills under her pillow, so the tooth fairy would exchange them for some unusual coins." he said.

I was beginning to feel a little bit like EBay, but I played along. The tooth fairy took the bills and left two unusual coins in exchange. All was well. The tooth fairy was prompt this time.

The next morning I awoke to the sounds of wailing children. The girls were crying because of the tooth fairy's visit. Apparently, Graceland left her money under her pillow against her will. She did not care for unusual coins, because she knew I would not let her spend them. Elvis had apparently forced her sister to leave the money under the pillow, and Graceland wanted her money back.

Although slightly annoyed, I could understand her position, but I could not understand why Elvis was also wailing. She finally calmed down enough to explain that she had left money under her pillow as well, but the tooth fairy didn't even touch it. Of course this meant that the tooth fairy had not left Elvis any coins. This puzzled Elvis since the whole exchange process had been her idea. Obviously, Graceland was an ungrateful recipient, and Elvis had been totally left out.

I suggested the two girls swap money with each other. They each would have the currency they wanted. Graceland liked this idea very much. Elvis did not. She explained that the tooth fairy very carefully hand selected just the right coin for each child. To go against the tooth fairy's wishes would just be WRONG.

With this proclamation, both girls resumed wailing. I sat them down and told them I had a plan. I explained to them where they went wrong by not leaving the tooth fairy a note explaining their wishes. Obviously the tooth fairy had been confused about what she was supposed to do. (The tooth fairy also needed an informant that did not omit so much information.) With this said, I wrote a note to the tooth fairy explaining the mix-up and how we hoped she could fix this problem. We put the note and money under the respective pillows in anticipation of the tooth fairy's next visit.

Luckily the tooth fairy remembered to come that night as well. The next morning, Graceland awoke to find her $2 back under her pillow, and Elvis found two unusual coins that had been selected just for her under her pillow. Finally the girls were happy.

However, when they saw what clothes I had picked out for them to wear that day, the wailing started all over again.

Lesson Learned: You should not expect the tooth fairy to change a dollar. Her business is tooth collecting, not coin collecting.

Bedroom Problems

When I was in first grade, my parents took me to Pittman's Furniture Store in Manchester, TN to pick out a new bedroom suite. They had decided that I no longer needed to sleep on my wagon wheel bunk bed. They felt that I needed something girlie.

We looked around the store, and my parents decided on the perfect bedroom suite for me. I hated it. I tried and tried to talk them out of buying it. I tried to show them a different less expensive bedroom suite. I repeatedly stressed to them about what an ugly shade of green it was. Because I obviously did not know what I needed and my parents did, they bought me the hideous 1970's green bedroom suit. They did not just buy a piece or two of the set. They bought the canopy bed, dresser, chest of drawers, desk, hutch, and chair with the ever-so-practical textured vinyl cushion.

Over the years, my mom told me how she would have felt like a princess if she had had a bed like mine. I always replied, "Would you like to have mine? Really, you can have it." This remark greatly annoyed her.

Years later when I got married, guess what my parents sent with me? My then new husband asked, "Do we have to keep this furniture?"

"Yes," I told him, "That bedroom suit is part of my never-ending punishment, but for what I do not know."

I had a plan, though. If we had a daughter, this bedroom furniture would become hers and would serve as her punishment for her misdeeds to come. "You have to be kidding." Doyle remarked. Yes, I was kidding. Maybe we could try to refinish all those ugly pieces of furniture. I had decided to let our "daughter-to-be" pick out the color we would use. (It would have to be painted, because staining it a wood color was only an unrealistic fantasy.)

Of course my husband and I ended up having two daughters. The oldest got most of the ugly bedroom furniture. Guess what? She loved it. In fact, our younger daughter loved it too. Since Graceland did not inherit the bed, we bought her a gorgeous wrought iron bed like the one in *My Fair Lady*. What did the then three year old say? "Why can't I have a bed like Elvis'?" One reason she cannot have a bed like that is because there is no way I would bring another bed like that into this house. I am afraid I will never get rid of the one we already have.

I did not say what kind of bed I now have as an adult. My husband bought it before we met. It has a wagon wheel at both ends. He is so proud of it. I think it somehow makes him feel connected to John Wayne, since it looks like it came straight out of an old western movie.

Lesson Learned: I shall never escape wagon wheels and ugly green beds.

Chapter 16
So Many Animal Problems

Slippery Frogs

In our first five years of marriage, my dad only came over to our house once or twice. After our first child was born, Pop came over every day after work. It made his reason for his visits pretty obvious, but it was good to see him so happy.

On one of Pop's evening visits, I noticed a toad outside our back door when Pop opened the door to leave. Precisely as I said, "Oh look - there's a toad," Pop stepped out the door. He looked back at me and asked, "Where?" As he took that big step down, he stepped smack dab on top of the toad, and his foot slid a few inches. As he slid, Pop grabbed the door frame to steady himself. Meanwhile, toddler Elvis asked, "Where's the toad?" I answered, "It's gone." (In the dead sense of the word) Pop asked, "Where did it go?" Pop had not looked under his shoe and had not figured out yet what had happened. (Doyle was just standing there too grossed out to say anything.) I again said, "The toad is Really Gone!" Dad kept pressing, "Which way did it go?!" Pop and Elvis peered all around the door step. Luckily Pop was still standing on it. Elvis wanted to go look for the toad. I said, "No it's dark outside, and it is time to brush Elvis' teeth." Doyle caught on to my distraction tactic and took Elvis away. I then explained to Pop what had happened to the toad. Pop was horrified and grossed out all at once.

A little later, Doyle relocated the toad. I asked no questions about the details of how he did it or where he took it. I decided a long time ago that it is a husband's job to dispose of all gross dead animals. This may sound sexist, but there it is. Take, for example, the lizards that our cats bring to the front door. The lizards are always missing their legs and tails. No matter how many times I say, "Bad kitty, Bad kitty!" those cats keep bringing us offerings. The headless snakes they bring are rather impressive, though. I cannot help but wonder if there was some sort of mongoose-style fight that preceded the snake's death. I also wonder if the cat was bitten and is about to die. That never happens, though. No matter what type of dead creature is found on our doorstep, my husband knows that it will lie there until he does something about it.

Lesson Learned: Little animals need to avoid our doorstep.

Dog Problems

When Elvis was almost three years old, she got a surprise package from Miss Ann, a friend who lives in California. Miss Ann sent Elvis a toy tape player with toy cassettes. Elvis started listening to the new toy while I went about my housework. After a half an hour or so of playing, she came looking for me, sobbing. It was obvious that she was heartbroken.

After much effort, I figured out that a song on one of the cassettes was what was upsetting her. The song was *Oh Where, Oh Where Has My Little Dog Gone?* I tried to explain that it was just a song, and that the singer had not really lost a dog. Elvis was not convinced and continued to sob for a good forty-five minutes.

I tried a distraction technique that had worked before. "Let's call Aunt Louise. Maybe she knows where the doggy went," I suggested.

Elvis thought that was a great idea. We called Aunt Louise, and she came up with a great answer. Aunt Louise always has stray animals coming to her house, so she said, "Sweetheart, that dog came to my house to live with all the other dogs."

That is all Elvis needed to hear. The crying stopped, and she ran off to play. She was not concerned at all that the singer of the song did not know where the dog was. What was important was that **Elvis** knew where the dog was.

Lesson Learned: Aunt Louise rocks!

Porsche Problems

Shortly after getting married, Doyle and I took in a feral kitten that we named Porsche. We had no idea that taming this cat should have been an impossible task. The only contact Porsche had had with human beings was when my Aunt Louise left food outside her house for this kitten and the kitten's wild family. Porsche was the only one in her family who would come close to the house or to Aunt Louise to eat.

Eventually we were able to pet Porsche occasionally, if we did not pet her head or tail or look at her the wrong way. At times, she would come into the house, but that was mainly to hide. Porsche was an OK pet as long as there were no children around. If there were children around, she hissed, swatted, and retreated.

When Elvis was about five years old, she began praying every night that God would make Porsche (now ten years old) "be nice". She prayed every night for two years for that cat.

When we moved to our new house, our now 12-year-old Porsche started acting like a new cat. She wanted to be petted by everyone and loved being held. She wanted to come in the house but did not hide like before. Porsche, our once child-hating cat, chose two year old Rebecca to be her favorite person.

After being amazed by her friendly behavior, one day I proclaimed, "What has gotten into this cat?" Elvis was totally disgusted with me. "Mom," she said, "Don't you remember? I pray for her every night!"

Lesson Learned: Forget the cat. I need to get Elvis to pray about bigger issues like world peace.

We Call Her Lassie

When we bought our new house, we were unaware that it came with a skunk and a feral cat. Our skunk, we soon found out, had the habit of spraying her stink under the house around 3:00 p.m. every day. Our house and everything in it took on the slight hint of eau de skunk. I burned candles; I washed clothes, but it was pointless.

The skunk also liked to spray into the drier vent. I would be ready to dry a load of wet clothes. I would open the drier door and wham! The smell would about knock me down. Even air drying the clothes did no good, because when 3:00 p.m. rolled around again, that skunk would issue a new installment of stink. It had become obvious that everyone and everything in our house was going to smell bad until we got rid of that skunk.

In the meantime, every cat in the neighborhood, including the wild cat that came with our new house, figured out how to use the cat door we had installed in the garage. The cats enjoyed the cat food we continuously poured into the food bowls. Apparently one of the many visiting cats had some contagious illness, and our sweet cat, Miata, caught it. This illness slowly killed Miata, and this devastated our children. Miata was the best natured cat I have ever had, and I have had more than a few cats.

Elvis decided that she would feel better about Miata's death if we got a new cat, but her daddy said, "No!" Porsche, our other cat, was finally acting nice and was obviously happy about Miata's absence. Doyle was afraid that another cat would drive Porsche back to her wild crazy ways. Elvis told me all about what she wanted her new cat to look like. I told her that her father mentioned that someday he wanted to have a solid gray cat like a cat he once had years earlier. I shared that the only cat we would come close to talking her father into would be a solid gray cat. This apparently sounded like a good idea to Elvis, so she convinced herself that she would like to have a gray cat, too. Elvis then asked her daddy for a solid gray cat. Shockingly he said, "No." "But Daddy, you want a gray cat." she declared. "I don't want any cat." he declared.

As the weeks went by, Elvis prayed every night that God would give her a gray kitten. In the meantime, I tried to talk Doyle into getting her a kitten. I told him about her prayers. He said, "If God wants her to have a gray kitten, He can get her a gray kitten!"

Christmas was drawing near. When asked what she wanted for Christmas, Elvis asked only for a gray kitten. I was afraid we were going to have another Christmas where Elvis asked for something we could not get her - like the magic carpet request from a few years earlier.

My mom and pop knew about Elvis's Christmas wish, as everyone else in the family did. One day at the college where my mom worked, a student asked Mom, "Do you know anyone who would like to have a kitten? I have several cats and most of them gang up on this 6 month old kitten. It has gotten so bad that I have to keep the kitten in a pet taxi for its own protection."

My mom asked, "What color is the kitten?" The girl thought that was an odd question. After all, cat's personalities are not dictated by their color. Isn't a cat's personality more important? (Not in my family.) The student replied, "She's all gray."

On Christmas day, my parents showed up at our house with a kitten. They told us the kitten was their new pet that they wanted to show us. My husband immediately knew he was being set up. I just stood back and smiled. He had said that if God wanted Elvis to have a gray kitten, He could get her one. Well, God got her one by using a student and my parents as helpers.

Mom insisted that she and Pop would be happy to keep the kitten at their house if we did not want it. Doyle would not give in, so Mom and Pop took the kitten home. Having two heartbroken little girls on Christmas Day turned out to be more than Doyle could take, and the next day, he told me to call my parents. The cat could be ours.

There was great celebrating at the Veazey house. The kitten was quickly named Harley Davidson, because that is what both Doyle and Elvis want to own someday. We could then also say that we had a Porsche and a Harley in our garage. I thought the kitten should be named "Rascal", because she thought my brand new curtains were for climbing and the new carpet was for pooping on.

Now back to the skunk, which continued to live under our house despite all our efforts to get rid of it. We found out how the skunk was getting under the house, so we put a live trap near the hole. We put all kinds of tempting skunk foods in that trap: tuna, raw eggs, etc. Apparently this skunk was very intelligent. She would not get into that trap.

We did, however, catch every cat in the neighborhood, including the feral cat. This half grown wild cat was hysterical in the trap and threw itself wildly against the cage. Large clumps of its fur were now gone. I was concerned that this cat was going to truly hurt itself, so I very unwisely let it go. (Yes, I did live to regret letting HER go, because she soon started having kittens.)

Each time I went outside to release another neighbor's cat, or the neighborhood possum, Harley ran over to me. She let out a continuous stream of short meows and insisted that I follow her. It was as if I were in a *Lassie* episode, and Harley had the role of Lassie. Pretending to be on the *Lassie* set, I would ask her things like, "Tommy is in a pit and needs our help?"

I occasionally stopped walking toward the trap and stood still. This really frustrated Harley, and she would walk back to me and meow repeatedly trying to urge me on. She would then resume walking toward the trapped animal, occasionally turning to see if I were following. I would again stop and act like I did not understand that I was supposed to follow. Finally when we got within sight of the trap, Harley stopped a safe distance from it and sat down triumphantly. She had saved the day again.

Lesson Learned: Quit letting Harley watch those *Lassie* reruns.

Allergy Problems

Harley is a sweet kitty, but she is not the sharpest knife in the drawer. Ever since she got trapped under the house for three days with numerous ant bombs going off, she has been even less intelligent. After the ant bomb incident, she also started losing patches of hair on her stomach. The vet believed the hair loss was unrelated to the ant bombs and said her problem was allergies. (I can only assume that she is allergic to our family.) This led to Harley receiving allergy shots.

One Friday after such a vet visit, we pulled into our driveway and let the traumatized cat out of the car. Nana soon arrived to take our two girls out for a little while. Doyle and I decided to take advantage of the opportunity and go out to dinner without whining children. I was driving, and as I backed out of the driveway, I felt a "Bloop". I had just run over Harley! I was so upset. I kept telling Harley, "I just took you to the vet. Couldn't you have run behind the car BEFORE I spent even more money on you?" The cat was making horrible noises as if she could not breathe. The vet's office was now closed for the weekend. I told Doyle to go get the gun. He kept saying, "Let's just wait a few minutes." I kept saying, "Wait a few minutes?! This stupid cat is suffering! Get the gun!"

We waited for what seemed like hours, but the cat's breathing started to sound more normal. Harley survived, amazingly, with no injuries that the vet could detect, except for even more clumps of missing fur and a tire tred mark across her stomach. I guess it was a good thing that Doyle did not get a gun after all. As for the horrible sounds that the cat was making, apparently she was having a panic attack. I can see how getting run over could cause panic.

For a time, this incident caused Harley to give up trying to lead our car down the driveway when we came home. She would call out to us, "Good luck finding the garage. You are on your own."

Lessons Learned: My car is kind to dumb animals, and ant bombs are not good for cats.

Wild Momma

The skunk must have gotten tired of all the other animals being trapped near her door/hole. (Can you imagine those poor trapped animals seeing that skunk walking around the outside of the trap, and them not being able to get away from her?) Anyway, the skunk moved out, and we plugged the hole under the house in case she changed her mind and came back.

In the meantime, we found out that our wild cat had had a litter of five kittens that she had kept hidden for about two months. These kittens were as wild as their momma. Our cat problems had now greatly multiplied. We came up with a grand plan to catch and tame all the kittens, and then find them new homes. (By the way, one of the kittens was gray. If you need any prayers answered, get Elvis to pray for you. Her prayers are very effective.)

After being hissed at constantly and scratched at ferociously, we realized the kittens were already too wild to domesticate. This created a new problem. No one wants feral female cats. Yes, three of these kittens were girls. Why couldn't the momma cat have had a small first litter like a normal cat?

I went ahead and advertised in the local paper that we had "free barn cats". We were able to give away one of the male kittens. Now I had to get serious about catching the female kittens. I once again pulled out the trusty live trap and caught them one by one. After I would catch a kitten, I would drive 15 miles to the cheapest vet around and have the girl kitty fixed. These wild kittens always screamed wildly during the car ride. The kittens did not meow like regular cats. They screamed like something out of a horror movie. (I suppose domestic cats learn to meow by listening to other cats.)

After I finally made it to the vet's office on one occasion, I jokingly asked the veterinarian if he could give me a sedative after my unnerving ride. He told me that the kitten needed it more than I did.

In the end I believe his opinion had changed. Each time I would pick up a newly-spayed kitten, he would tell me about how horribly wild that kitten was, and what a hard time he had with her. This led me to wonder. Who needed the sedative more, Doc? You or the kitten?

The wild cat, Wild Momma as we called her, had figured out how to stay away from our trap no matter what food we had in it. Male cats hung out constantly at our house, and I knew why. Wild Momma had had so many kittens in her first litter, I was afraid of how many kittens she would have next time. We did not want to have to pay to spay yet another litter. Wild Momma would have to be fixed.

I was beginning to stress about the situation. Those male cats were not just after Wild Momma. They were also harassing Porsche and Harley. Porsche was very much offended by the whole situation, and Harley was horrified. I thought I was going to have to give Harley sedatives. The visiting boy cats did not know or care that both our girl cats had been fixed.

I was at my wit's end by this point. I feared the feral cat was already pregnant for the second time. I needed help from above, so I began to pray about it. I really believe God gave me the idea to use a pet taxi to catch that cat. Wild Momma had never been in or even seen a pet taxi as far as I knew.

The day had come for me to try to catch Wild Momma. I hoped to have everything settled by the time I had to leave for choir practice in the evening. I am notorious for arriving late to choir, but I felt confident that this night would be different.

I set out the food-filled pet taxi in the yard. I waited in hiding all afternoon. The cat did not go near that pet taxi.

The day dragged on. I waited and waited. It was now time to leave for choir practice, and still the cat had not appeared. I was running out of time but did not want to give up on my watch.

Finally, I gave up. Choir practice had already started, and the pet taxi was still vacant. I gave up my hiding place and went into the house. As soon as I shut the front door and glanced out the window, I saw Wild Momma get into the pet taxi. I ran out the back door, snuck around the house, and approached the pet taxi from behind.

I slammed the taxi door shut, and Wild Momma went wild. She had to spend the night in the pet taxi before visiting the vet. Once Wild Momma was spayed, I had no trouble finding a horse barn for her to call home. (Catching her again was a different story, and Doyle has the scars to prove it.) And though the farmer told me he would return the cat if things did not work out, I knew that was an idle threat. No one would ever catch that cat again.

Now we were down to only one wild, boy kitten. Once again I advertised in the newspaper but had no takers. I also prayed that God would help me get rid of this wild kitten. In the meantime, Doyle had been cutting up fallen trees on our property. We had had a bad ice storm and had lost several trees. We do not have a fireplace, so Doyle just stacked up the firewood he had cut. He planned to give it to anyone who needed it.

One day, two teenagers drove up. One came to our door to ask about the firewood. He said his father had told his brother and him to go out and cut firewood for the winter. Instead, the two brothers decided to drive around and see if they could find some wood that no one wanted. (I wonder how much wood they could have chopped in the amount of time they spent driving around.) As he and I were talking, Graceland came outside to see what was going on. The boy commented about one of our cats. Graceland asked, "You're not going to take one of our kitties are you?" (My girls were not happy about giving away those wild cats.) The boy laughed and said, "We don't need a pet. We need a barn cat."

"Oh really?" I said, "I'll tell you what. If you take one of our barn cats, you can have that big stack of firewood for free."

He was so proud that his lazy plan worked. I was so proud that he fell for mine. We were getting rid of a stack of unwanted wood and the last feral cat.

Lesson Learned: Wild cats can bite through leather gloves and praying really does work.

Chester Problems

We decided years ago that if you like unusual names, you should stick them on your pets, not your children. For this reason, our animals always have unique names.

For several years, we stuck with one theme for pet names, expensive rides. We have had cats named Porsche, Miata, Mercedes, and Harley Davidson. We had to nickname Mercedes, "Mercy", because that is what that poor kitty needed with small children around.

Because we always have several cats, mice are not problems at our house. There is frequently a mouse "offering" or "present" for the family at the doorstep. I always tell the cats what bad kitties they are. This seems to only make them try harder. Now don't lecture me on how I am hurting the cats' psyche, because it hurts my psyche to see such a sight. I have this fear of stepping out my door one day and my foot landing on something mutilated and dead, or worse yet my foot landing on something mutilated and not quite dead.

One day Harley caught a mouse. She had not killed it but turned it loose in the garage. I was now having flashbacks to my childhood, and how our cats never would finish killing their prey. My children were horrified, so we rescued the mouse. It was the ugliest mouse I had ever seen. As it turns out, it was not a mouse, mole, or vole. I think it was a shrew.

My daughters named the creature "Chester". I believe that was a name that came from a book that

Elvis was reading at the time. We gathered the cats and locked them up. We then were able to take Chester out into the woods and set him free. All was now well in the world.

The next day, we came home to find Chester dead at the back door. Elvis sobbed. I tried to console her by saying, "Maybe it's not Chester." "But it looks like him." Elvis insisted. This creature did look just as weird as the other thing had, so Elvis had a good point. "Maybe this one is a different mouse from Chester's family." I reassured her. (I do not know why I thought saying that would help.) Now Graceland started sobbing. "What's wrong with you?" I asked. "That's probably his baby sister!" Graceland cried. Being the baby sister of our family, this scenario was much worse to Graceland than if this dead animal were Chester himself.

Because of the death, we had to have a funeral. Our cats tried to join in with what was going on. This only caused angry tears on the part of my daughters, who were now calling the cats "murderers" and "mouse killers". They made my "bad kitty, bad kitty" calls sound like sweet pet names. The cats realized that they were now despised pets. I think it was because of this that for the next week and a half, a dead member of Chester's family awaited us when we got home at the end of each day. Apparently Chester's entire family was now wiped out. You can imagine the hysteria I had to face every day. I finally wised up and sent the girls in through the front door and avoided the garage door altogether, since that was the favorite dead critter drop off spot.

I had to run and check the garage door steps before the girls went out to get their bikes. Luckily the cats always left their "presents" on the door mat. This made for an easy cleanup. I would grab opposite sides of the mat and pray that the animal did not roll up against me. I carefully carried the carcass to the woods where I respectfully tossed him into the leaves. Tossing out dead animals is supposed to be my husband's job, but I did not want to go through all the drama of another "dead Chester" burial.

Lesson Learned: If you are a rodent family, and you are losing family members on a daily basis, maybe you should move away from the house with all the cats.

Snake Problems

One day Graceland came running into the house. I thought she had been given the gift of speaking in tongues, because I could not understand a word she said. Then I thought Elvis had been given the gift of interpretation when she translated for her sister. Elvis said, "She said there is a black snake in the back yard!" Eek! I hate snakes, and evidently Graceland does, too. I did not want some snake sliding around in the yard. What if it were poisonous?

I went into the backyard armed with a can of mace in one hand and a shovel in the other. My plan was to stun it and then whack it. My girls stayed inside, with their noses pressed against the window panes, watching my every move. Talk about pressure! Sweat was pouring down my back. I was afraid I would actually find the snake just as it was biting me. Then my girls would watch their mother die of a heart attack before the venom could even affect me.

No snake was found, so I made the girls stay in the house for the rest of the day. A week or so later, Graceland came running into the bathroom, bringing me a snake skin that she had found in our side yard next to the house. Eek! Yes, I was "using" the bathroom at that particular moment. Talk about a captive audience. I told her, "Put that thing down and wash your hands!" Graceland looked surprised that I appeared so upset. She then laid the skin next to me and stepped over to the sink. Grossed out by what was now next to me, I excitedly proclaimed, "Take that thing back outside." She continued over to the sink. I said, "Don't wash your hands (since she was just going to pick that thing up again.)" Graceland just stood at the sink looking back at me. She had her hands over the sink and the water running, but she stood there doing nothing. She looked at me as if I had truly finally gone "over the edge". I think she was waiting for me to change my mind again about what she should be doing. Finally I calmly said, "Forget about washing your hands right now. Just take that skin outside then come right back and wash your hands." You could tell that Graceland considered these nonconflicting directions much easier to follow.

Graceland had found the snake skin beside our house. Its owner was probably calmly shedding it beside the house while I was combing the back yard wanting to kill it a week earlier.

Lesson Learned: Snakes really do "creep me out".

Demon Kitty Problems

Our cat, Porsche, was getting old and feeble. When I took her to the vet, he said he was fairly certain that she had a tumor in her abdomen. She acted so horribly, however that the vet could not thoroughly examine her. He finally just declared, "This cat is CRAZY", and gave up on the examination.

Since my children had cried for two years over Miata's death, I decided to be more proactive this time. I thought Porsche's days were numbered, so perhaps we should go ahead and get a replacement cat. I did not need to suggest this idea to my children, because Graceland was always asking for a kitten of her own. She wanted a calico, and she wanted to name her Cali. She came up with this idea on her own, which I thought was pretty creative for a 5-year-old.

As luck would have it, my dear friend Bobbie, also known as BFF Bobbie, owned a cat that had just had kittens. She was proud to tell me that one kitten was a calico. When the kittens were only a few weeks old, Graceland and I visited Miss Bobbie. It turned out that this kitten was a motley kitten. She was extremely ugly to me, but gorgeous to Graceland. Of course Graceland wanted to take the kitten home, but I repeatedly told her that the kitten was too young to leave her mother.

As we went home, Graceland sobbed, "I'm going to miss Cali!" I told her she would have to talk to her daddy about getting another cat. I warned her not to cry in front of Daddy about the kitten, because tears do not soften Doyle's heart. In fact, they have the opposite effect.

When Doyle got home from work, Graceland started telling him about Cali. Then she bolted to her room to secretly cry. After regaining her composure, she came back into the kitchen and resumed talking to her father about the kitten. She again got too emotional, because Daddy was not acting like he cared for the idea at all. Once again, Graceland ran out of the kitchen in mid-sentence. This charging and retreating happened several times that evening. Doyle would look at me as if to say, "Why does she keep running out of the room in mid-sentence?" I innocently shrug my shoulders.

After Graceland and Elvis went to bed, I worked on Doyle. He did not put up too much of a fight. It only took a few weeks of begging. I suspect that compared to Elvis' request for a pet wolf, a kitten did not sound so bad.

I took Graceland to Miss Bobbie's house after preschool when the kittens were old enough to find a new home. Graceland thought we were just going for a visit. She did not know there was a pet taxi hidden in the trunk of the car for our return trip. After Graceland had loved on Cali for some time, I brought in the pet taxi. I don't think Graceland was getting her hopes up enough to suppose that we were going to keep Cali for more than a day or two. Once Doyle gave Graceland his "OK" later that night, she finally allowed herself to get excited, and excited she was.

I thought this kitten was going to be such a sweet addition to our family. I was wrong.

Graceland stuck with the name Cali for the kitten, but I preferred "Demon Kitty". I also thought "Cato" was a good choice. Cato was the character in the Pink Panther movies who attacked Inspector Clouseau when the inspector least expected it. After he attacked, Cato would not stop attacking.

This is a pretty accurate description of our new demon kitty. She attacked everyone and everything, especially Graceland (talk about biting the hand that feeds you). Even our two grown cats were horrified by her. Because they never knew when "Demon Kitty" was going to attack, they crouched as they walked around the house and growled all the time while constantly looking from left to right. In this way, they always looked and sounded ready for an attack.

The day of her most vicious attack was also the day Demon Kitty was scheduled to go to the vet. She mercilessly attacked Graceland's leg and would not let go. One advantage to this was that the kitten was easier to catch. Once I had her in my clutches, I think she knew she had really messed up. I could read that in her little yellow eyes. I wore her out with a newspaper, stuffed her in the pet taxi, and took her for the long drive to our vet's office, where she was spayed.

Lesson Demon Kitty thought she learned: If you mess with the Veazey children, Karen will have the vet remove one of your organs!

Sassy Pants

Because some people like to dump unwanted animals in the country, my Aunt Louise occasionally has a new furry friend show up at her house. During some extremely hot summer days that we were having here in Tennessee one August, a young momma cat and two kittens showed up at Aunt Louise's door. They were all in terrible shape and obviously had not eaten in a while.

As always, Aunt Louise fed the poor things and wondered why they would not go away. A few days later, Aunt Louise found one of the kittens dead. Two days after that, Aunt Louise noticed that the other kitten was now missing. She knew that both kittens were sickly, and she assumed the second kitten had suffered the same fate.

This led Aunt Louise to take her usual course of action. She called me and asked when I was going to come and get the momma cat. I am not sure why this situation was deemed to be my problem, but I reminded Aunt Louise that we already had three cats. I also reminded her that one of our cats had come from her house during a similar situation.

My girls were very sad to hear about the kittens. I was not aware of it, but Elvis, the prayer warrior, started praying about the missing kitten. The next morning was a Saturday, and I was getting ready to go to work. Elvis came running down the stairs and shouted, "God told me that the kitten is not dead, but we only have until noon to find her, or she will be dead. He also said I cannot eat until after we find her, dead or alive."

Elvis did not know anything about fasting, so I knew she wasn't making that part up. I told her, "I can't take you to Aunt Louise's. I have to go to work." I turned to my husband. He said, "She's going to go hungry, because I have things to do."

Well Elvis went hungry, but Doyle finally gave in. Doyle, Elvis, and Graceland made it to Aunt Louise's house at the lake at 10:30 am. The three of them searched and searched. At 11:50a.m. Doyle spotted the kitten deep in a rocky ravine. Elvis climbed down and rescued the kitten, which was apparently unable to climb out of the ravine. Because of the 105-degree temperature, no food, and no water, the kitten was in bad shape. Once up to the house, Doyle, our girls, and Aunt Louise started trying to nurse the kitten back to health.

I believe that Aunt Louise secretly loves nursing little creatures back to health, so she decided to keep the kitten in the house until it was well. Two days later, our girls insisted that we go over to see the kitten after school. I called Aunt Louise, and she told me that the kitten was still unable to use its back legs. Aunt Louise reported that she had also found two puncture wounds on one thigh and assumed the kitten had been bitten by something poisonous. Aunt Louise said she was taking the kitten to the vet to have it put down.

I picked my girls up from school, and they talked excitedly about seeing the kitten. I told them that we would go to Aunt Louise's, but that the kitten would probably be dead before we got there. Elvis calmly said, "Mom, God told me that the kitten is going to be fine." I thought, "The vet may not have heard that."

Once at Aunt Louise's house, I asked, "Did you put the kitten down?" Aunt Louise said, "No, the vet said that both back legs are broken near the hips. One break is a very bad compound fracture, and the bone has splintered. The vet said that that leg will probably have to be amputated at the hip." I could tell by the look in her eye what Aunt Louise was thinking. "You cannot seriously think that I am going to take a three-legged cat off your hands?" I asked.

Aunt Louise was shocked. Not only did she expect me to take a three-legged cat off her hands, but she expected me to take that cat's momma off her hands as well. I repeatedly said, "We need to just put the kitten down." Elvis repeatedly said, "Mom, God told me the kitten is going to be fine."

Aunt Louise spent the next four weeks giving the kitten antibiotics and other medications two to three times a day. In addition to having a serious infection where the compound fracture had punctured threw the skin, both the kitten's eyes were infected. Aunt Louise had to confine the kitten to a pet taxi to limit its mobility, so its bones could heal. By now we had discovered that the kitten was a "she".

Meanwhile, our girls tried to talk Doyle and me into adopting at least the kitten if not the mother, too. I said I might be willing to take the kitten if we named her "Gimpy". Our girls were horrified, and objected. I said, "You can't have her, then."

After four weeks of Aunt Louise's rehabilitation efforts, guess who came to live with us. Amazingly, her leg did not have to be amputated, and she does not even have a slight limp. The only time you might suspect she had a problem was when she tried to quickly make a 360 degree turn. She always fell over and looked around to see who she can blame. Because she didn't limp, we could not name her Gimpy, so we eventually agreed on "Sassy Pants". Well, we did not **all** agree. Elvis insisted on calling her "Rascal". This name was also totally appropriate. The kitten was unbelievably playful and loved to be carried around if you laid her over your left shoulder. She enjoyed sitting in Graceland's doll highchair while eating Kitten Chow. She also seemed to enjoy being dressed up in doll clothes and carried around in a doll carrier. She was going to be a great pet for our girls.

What about the mother cat? Aunt Louise got stuck with her. Hee Hee!

Lesson Learned: Before you put an animal "down", check with Elvis. She may have heard of some "higher" plans.

Conclusion

I hope you have enjoyed reading about the lessons I have learned. I will leave you with one final lesson.

The Big Lesson Learned: Life really can be a sitcom. All you have to do is search for the humor in whatever awkward or unfortunate situation you find yourself. There may come a time when you cannot find any humor in a situation. It is times like these that you have to give yourself permission to have amnesia.

Made in the USA
Lexington, KY
10 February 2015